# Acting means <u>Doing</u> !!

*Here are all the Techniques you need, carrying you confidently
from Auditions through Rehearsals - Blocking, Characterization -
into Performances, all the way to Curtain Calls*

by Jim Cavanaugh

Cover Design by Jane Goodman Pollak


First Edition

ISBN-13: 978-1477491591
ISBN-10: 1477491597

Jim Cavanaugh
1204 Defford Lane
Allen TX 75002

cavanaughjt@gmail.com

www.acting-means-doing.com
www.actingmeansdoing.com

For my children,
Kathleen and Brennan,
as I've dedicated with love
every worthwhile thing I've done
in their lifetimes.

Jim Cavanaugh is Emeritus Professor of Theatre Arts at Mount Holyoke College, South Hadley, Massachusetts, where for 23 years he taught Acting and Directing, and seminars on contemporary theatre – and directed 38 productions.

He also founded and produced the Mount Holyoke College Summer Theatre, directing 46 plays, and acting in 28 under other directors.

Jim studied directing with Lee Strasberg at the American Theatre Wing in New York, and holds a Bachelor of Fine Arts degree from the Goodman Memorial Theatre and School of Drama, of the Art Institute of Chicago, which was awarded him with High Honors in Directing.

On Broadway, he acted in one play and stage managed two musicals and, one year, the Tony Awards.  He directed two plays off-Broadway.

In community theatres in Rochester (MN), Omaha, and Heidelberg, Germany, he directed a total of 70 plays.  He was one of the earliest to be honored as a 'Fellow' by the American Community Theatre Association (now the American Association of Community Theatres), on whose Board of Directors he served a long stint, and was a frequent adjudicator of performances at their state and regional theatre festivals.

Earlier, in professional summer theatres from Sacramento to Chicago to Rangeley (ME), Jim acted, directed, stage managed, and designed lighting. At NBC in New York, he directed at the Radio Workshop.

His previous books are "Organization and Management of the Non-Professional Theatre," and "Theatre for the Community: Organizational Structure."  Jim reviewed many theatre manuscripts for Schirmer Books, and for that publisher helped complete the final work of the Dean of Broadway Musical Directors, Lehman Engel, "Getting the Show On."

He began his theatre work at age fourteen with the Augusta (GA) Players, a community theatre for which his first assignment was to sit for several hours each day over a hot-plate in the orchestra pit (because that's where the only household wall plug was located) stirring a double-boiler containing the evil-smelling "sizing" which was then mixed with pigment paint, allowing it to adhere to the canvas scenery.  The odors that clung irrevocably to his clothing and his skin removed forever any illusions about the glamour of a life in the theatre.

I deplore, as perhaps you do, the continued inexplicable use today of the long-traditional Royal "he," as an all-inclusive personal pronoun, regardless of the gender of the individual or the group being discussed.

[e.g. "On the night before Graduation, every student stayed up as late as he possibly could" was written not long ago about a co-ed school (*).]

In this book, I've been pretty successful in avoiding that gender-general passé male pronoun (as well as its equally thoughtless cousins, "his" and "him"), and the supposedly politically-correct "he or she" and "s/he," which stand out as vividly and artificially on a page as "flesh-colored" bandages do on skinned knees.

Oh, you'll catch me backsliding a few times herein, but when those tetchy chaperones, Grammar and Usage and Syntax, have made it necessary to use "He" to refer to a person under discussion, you can be sure that pretty quickly a "She" will appear in a similar representative role.

(*) All such bad examples found in this book - largely of theatre performances - were at one time seen or heard or read by the author. There are *good* examples, too, but they're rarely as interesting.

# ACKNOWLEDGEMENTS

When Richard Burton was playing Hamlet on Broadway, a friend was startled to see him drain a large glass of Scotch whisky before going on stage. When asked about it, Burton is reputed to have said: "You can't expect me to go out there *alone*!!"

No more could I have written this book *alone*.

No, I had by my side the memories of theatre colleagues whose companionship and fine work through the years inspired me to do ever better as an actor, director and teacher - and whose guidance, implicit and explicit, helped me along the road to accomplish that.

Way back at the beginning, Patience Hurd Middleton, Edmund C. Wilkes and Beth Stanfield showed me how to build the base on which all future learning and experience could settle in and find nourishment.

In my four years at the Goodman Theatre School of Drama, I was fortunate to be a student both before and after the torch was passed from the inspiring old guard (Maurice Gnesin, David Itkin, Walter Martini, and Mary Agnes Doyle) to the innovative new (John Reich and Charles McGaw) as the magnificent Bella Itkin continued during both regimes.

I owe enormous Thanks to these shapers of my very rough early abilities, as well as to the hundreds and hundreds of actors and directors and students I've been privileged to work alongside since, in our blessed art form, in theatres large and small, and productions lavish and scrawny.

Most recently and of the greatest value was a several-day visit from three former students and colleagues, now all successful professionals, who suggested (nay, demanded) that I curtail "making the rounds" of literary agents and publish this blasted book myself. And like the Little Red Hen, I did. For their advice and counsel throughout the whole process, I am deeply, deeply indebted to Courtney Flanagan, of the Theatre Faculty at The Bishop's School in San Diego; Paul Gregory, President of Focus Lighting in New York and around the world; and Michael Walker, actor, director, producer and playwright. Very simply, this book would not have seen the light of day without their warmhearted, strong and very welcome support.

Specific gratitude goes to my one-time students and fellow company members Susan Daniels, now a theatre teacher herself, who gave this book its working title ("An Actor's Technique"), and actor/director/ playwright/ producer Jack Neary, who shared his experiences in the initial serpentine process of formatting a manuscript for self-publishing, and Jane Goodman Pollak, nationally-respected author, speaker and lifestyle entrepreneur, who, long after her days of designing spot-on and beautiful logos for my academic-year and summer theatre productions, returned to bring her artist's eye and deft touch to design this book's cover. They offered the strength of their moral support as the volume was taking shape.

In accordance with the recurring theme of "I couldn't have done it by myself," I give grateful thanks to these actors, associates, or former students of mine, who each wrote a magnificent letter on my behalf – in vain – to persuade literary agents that, tho I don't number movie stars among my graduates, this book isn't aimed at stardom, but seeks instead to provide a solid basic technique for the craft of acting: Paula T. Alekson, Allen Bonde, Michael Brindisi, Carolyn L. Buck, Susan Buckley, Barbara Bunyan, Deirdre D. Budzyna, John Budzyna, Deb Guston, Dr. Linda Kodesch, Lindsay Reading Korth, Robert E. Leonard, Dr. Margaret Maytan, Catherine A. Moore, Dr. St. Elmo Newton, Bess O'Brien, Nancy D. Perkins, Dr. Stephen N. Rous, Sandy Shinner, Barbara B. Smith, Jennifer Wirth Symington, and the incomparable Louis Zorich.

I received sound and helpful advice from my children, Kathleen Cavanaugh Huss and Brennan Cavanaugh, and from theatre friends since our high-school days, Joan Bennett Harris and Jack Conyers – and Jack's keen-eyed, well-spoken wife (whom he met in a theatre!) Billie Conyers.

And a grandfather-author's warm and loving thanks go to the talented Samantha Huss, for drawing the fine sketches.

To them and to all my colleagues in a lifetime of classes, rehearsals, openings, and performances: I'm so grateful that I wasn't *alone* while reassembling these techniques that guided our paths and saved our skins many a time.

But the memories of these folks' influence on me would still be locked in my heart and my head, without the patience and skills of Jon Roundy, president of High Tech Nation, the computer guru who took my loose pages and adeptly turned them into this book.

Thank You, all.

# TABLE OF CONTENTS

.

# Chapter 1

# Glossary

of

## Theatre Terms
## useful to actors

These are offered to you here, up front, instead of buried somewhere in an appendix in the back, so you can wander through them now at your own speed, spotting some familiar backstage vocabulary as well as words and phrases that are new, and maybe useful, to you.

All of these terms are discussed at greater length, throughout the book.

**Above** – **Upstage** of an object.

**Accent** – The vocal stress put upon a word or syllable as emphasis. (Not to be confused with **Dialect**)

**Acting** – The portrayal of the inner life of a character as gracefully and efficiently as possible. i.e. **Doing**.

**Actor** – The theatrical performer who, with grace, efficiency, and technique, brings a character alive on stage, and the person for whom this book is written. (The term "Actress" seems to have disappeared in recent years.)

**Actor's Energy** – The extra vitality brought to the stage that sets your performance above and apart from the more subdued everyday pace and intensity of "real life."

**Ad lib** – (Latin: *ad libitum* = At [your] pleasure.)  Improvised dialogue, to fill a gap when someone has forgotten a line, or a scenic, prop, lighting or costume disaster has occurred; or (unforgivably) to show off.  The "pleasure" should be the audience's, not an egotistic performer's.

**Applause** – That very welcome response when the audience claps their hands to acknowledge something onstage that has pleased them, a lot.

**Apron** – The **Stage** floor extending in front of the **Proscenium Arch,** extending the acting area.  Announcements may be made out here, or whole scenes may be set, with the main curtain closed behind them.

**Arena Theatre** – Theatre-in-the-Round, with the stage in the middle of the **House**, and the audience arranged 360 degrees around it.  Some theatres produce their plays in this arrangement because they like the nearness of the audience, some because their performance space won't allow a **Proscenium Stage**, and some because of the money saved by the elimination of full-scale scenery.

**Aside** – Line(s) which the actor speaks directly toward the audience, usually with the accepted convention that the other characters can't hear him.

**Audience** – The good people for whom we spend all those hours, rehearsing and performing.  The patient folks who sit in the House and listen and laugh and applaud (and keep very quiet during our best dramatic moments) so we may ply our craft for them.

**Auditions** – Often called "Tryouts," at which actors, singers and dancers demonstrate their abilities to perform in an upcoming production, for the delectation of a director or casting director, who's watching and taking notes.

**Backstage** – Everyplace in the theatre behind the scenery, or acting area of the stage. Usually includes scene and costume shops, dressing rooms, Green Room, etc.

**Balances** – Equal vocal stress given to two ideas in a line of dialogue, e.g. "I <u>told</u> him, and then I <u>kicked</u> him."

**Below** – **Downstage** of an object.

**Bit** – A piece of stage Business, usually comedic. Obviously its use in theatre parlance parallels its usual definition: "A small portion." The word is used in situations like: "Let's rehearse that bit where you avoid tripping over the coffee table," and "That sticky-fingered bit where you can't let go of the dollar bill is hilarious."
   "Bit" can also refer to a small role in the play.

**Black Box** – A simple performance space, able to be configured into any physical set-up of audience-actor relationship, usually created by a theatre organization that already has a larger "Main Stage," wanting a smaller venue for experimental productions. New, financially-limited theatres will often begin in this basic, inexpensive set-up.

**Blackout** – The sudden extinguishing of all stage lights at once, instead of closing the curtain, often as a sudden punctuation to the final line of a scene, especially if it's a comic line or a frightening turn in a mystery.

**Blocking** – Every movement you make on stage, as discovered by trial and error in rehearsal, or by the dictates of the director. All blocking is written into the master script by the Stage Manager, thus becoming the physical pattern of the performance.

**Boards** – A traditional term for the Stage. "I trod the boards for forty years," you may hear an old actor say with a reminiscent smile.

**The Book** – Actor's jargon for the Script. "Will you hold book for me?" means "I think I know my lines on these pages, so will you follow me in the script, and correct me?"

**Box Set** – Scenery consisting of three walls, presented as ¾ of a square box, with the "Fourth Wall" removed, so the paying customers can see what's happening. The term is mostly used for scenery depicting a room.

**Break up** – The unforgiveable sin of an actor losing concentration because of, e.g., an onstage error or unexpected sound offstage or in the House, causing the performer to smile, or, worse, to laugh out loud.

**Business** – Any activity engaging the actor, from frying eggs to tying shoes to hugging to slapping to painting to sneezing to reading to writing to throwing to drinking, to falling on the floor, et al.

**Button** - The crisp, clean, certain ending to a Laugh Line, giving it closure, and inviting the laugh.

**Calls** – The announcements the Stage Manager makes to the cast and crew backstage before each performance (Usually "One Hour," "Half Hour," "15 minutes," "5 minutes," and "Places") and during each intermission (Usually: "5 minutes," and "Places.")

**Call Board** – Backstage bulletin board, containing Rehearsal schedules, notices of costume fittings, meetings, etc. This is usually where the cast and crew <u>sign in</u> upon arrival at the Theatre.

**Call Time** (or **Check-in** or **Sign-in Time**) – The moment when you are due in the theatre, for rehearsal or performance. Disregard it at your peril. If you're not 10 minutes early, you're 10 minutes Late, because a great many people are depending on you.

In professional theatre, this is traditionally a Half-Hour before Curtain, but most non-professional groups want the cast on site an hour, or hour-and-a-half, before the time the play has been advertised to begin.

**Cast** – All of the actors in the play.  As a verb, it means to assign those actors to their roles, often by a Casting Director.

**Character** – The person in the script whom you are playing, creating in Rehearsal that person's voice, and way of standing, walking, handling Props, etc.  When you are in full-out portrayal mode, you're said to be "<u>In</u> Character."

**Cheat** – To turn your face slightly **Downstage**, so the audience can better see you and hear your voice, even if it may seem to you unnatural not to be facing your conversational partner directly.

**"Chinese Arched Bridge"** – A helpful image to use during a Transition.  Going up the rising approach to the Bridge, you're moving out of the previous Emotion, experiencing the Transition at the top and, going down the other side, moving into the New emotion.

**Choice** – (also called the **Decision**) is usually the stimulus toward, or the direct result of, a Transition. This is the instant the Audience is aware that you have Chosen to leave the room, to kiss the nursemaid, to hit the bully, to mix a drink, or simply to sit down or stand up.  Your progress through the play is marked by a series of Choices, that you (or you in partnership with your director) have made in rehearsal.

**Climax** – The point of greatest intensity, the high point, of the play; the satisfying of the conflict that drove the plot.

**Concentration** – Total focus on the Moment at hand, shutting out your offstage life, and any nearby random noises or movements. Your cues, your lines, your blocking, your character, your emotion occupy you completely.

**Concept** – The Idea that the Playwright hopes to instill in the audience's mind or viscera, through the medium of the Play.  It's the director's happy responsibility to discern this Concept, and serve as the go-between from the Playwright to the Audience, using all the

Arts of the Theatre as tools.  And your work as an actor helps your director to realize the Concept.

**Convention** – an atypical technique in performance, accepted jointly by the actor and the audience, such as the Aside; everyone speaking English, though the play is set in Outer Mongolia; and the furniture in the living room all more or less facing in the same direction, out toward the audience, unnatural but necessary.

**Costume** – The clothing worn by your character in the play, as designed or chosen by the Costume Designer, whether it's a Roman toga or a cocktail dress.

**Counting the House** – Looking directly into the audience, and thereby disrupting the believability of the world Onstage.  It takes its name from the old days of the actor-manager, who was literally tabulating the number of audience members while rattling off the play's dialogue, to be sure the Box Office staff was reporting an honest total of ticket sales.

**Covering** – Standing directly downstage of, and therefore hiding, another actor from the audience.  Not nice.

**Crew** – The unseen people who make the technical aspects of the show work.  During performance, these will be the Running Crews, in Sets, Costumes, Props, Lighting, and Sound, each of which is composed of from one to many hard workers.  In the weeks before the show opens, the Preparation Crews will be busy in each of these areas.

**Cross** – walking from one location on stage to another.  Often indicated in a script as: "X".  [A **Counter-cross** occurs when Actor #1 crosses below Actor #2, who at the same time or immediately afterward, crosses toward the spot Actor #1 has vacated.  Often they virtually have changed places.]

**Cue** – A signal for action, given by the **Stage Manager** to one or more of the Crews: Lights, Sound, Curtain, etc.

Also: The final words or syllables of an actor's speech - or a sound or piece of business - which "cues" another actor to begin speaking. (In this regard, when learning lines actors often ask friends or other actors to "cue" them, saying the previous line before each of their lines.)

**Curtain** – The drapery hanging inside the Proscenium Arch, hiding the stage, the scenery and the actors until it is raised, or parted, when the play, and each subsequent act, begins.

**Curtain (Curtain Time) (Curtain Up) (Ring Up)** - The moment when each act of the play begins.

**Curtain Call** – At the end of the play, the entire cast gathers on stage to bow, acknowledging the applause of the audience.

**Curvilinear** – The arc-shaped movements that characterize a Comedy: softer, rounder lines of scenery and costume, and walking and handling Props, than in a Drama.

**Decision** – See Choice.

**Dialect** – The regional manner of speech used by a character in the play; e.g., Brooklyn, Southern, British, Irish, German, etc. Not to be confused with **Accent**, which refers to vocal emphases.

**Dialogue (or Dialog)** – The lines in the script, to be spoken by the actors.

**Director** - The person who interprets the script and finds its Concept, then casts and rehearses the actors to bring that concept to life, and melds the designers (scenery, costume, lighting, and sometimes sound) into a unified team to communicate that interpretation to the audience.

**Discovered** – When the curtain rises or the lights go up, beginning a scene, the actors already on stage are said to be "Discovered."

**Downstage** – The portion of the stage closest to the audience.

**Dress Rehearsal(s)** – The final rehearsals before Opening Night, when all the design and technical aspects of the production are added: Scenery, Costumes, Make-up, Lighting, Sound, etc.

**Dry** – Forgetting your lines.  (See also **Go Up**)

**Ensemble** – The all-for-one camaraderie that is engendered among the happiest companies, casts and crews.  This working together in harmony creates tighter and smoother performances, which an audience senses and responds to positively.

**Entrance (Enter)** – The actor goes onto the stage, in view of the audience.

**Ethnocentricity** – The belief that you and your group are superior to all others.  In the Theatre, this too often occurs when actors (for example) feel that the wardrobe and prop crews are there to serve them, and the crews feel that the actors are dimwits who mishandle the costumes and the props.  And set designers disdain actors who stand in front of the scenery, blocking it from the audience's view.
**Wrong – Wrong – All Wrong!**  (See **Ensemble,** for the correct antidote to **Ethnocentricity.**)

**Exit** – The actor leaves the stage. (From the Latin for "He goes out."  In many old scripts you'll find the term **"Exeunt."** (Latin for **"**They go out."**)**

**Exposition** – Telling the audience the Backstory of the play, as much as they need to know to follow the ensuing plot, usually in the first few minutes of Act I, and the first lines of each entering character.  The better playwrights create dialogue that presents Exposition so smoothly, and the better actors say those lines so interestingly, that the audience members don't realize that they're being handed bald-faced Information.

**Eye Contact** – Two actors locking eyes with each other, which gives the audience a stronger belief in their relationship – at the same time creating a strong bond between the actors to help each in building that relationship within the play, together.

**Farce** – A broad comedy characterized by a great deal of physical action, often slapstick: slamming doors, falling down, running across the stage, bumping into each other, being swatted with a rubber chicken, etc.

**"Find your Light"** – A skillful actor's challenge to slightly adjust the blocking, to be more directly lit by the beam of a stage light.

**Flat** – The basic unit of scenery in a Box Set, usually rectangular, joined together with other flats to create a semi-realistic room, usually on a Proscenium Stage.  With more and more theatres producing on Arena or Thrust Stages, flats have largely given way to more three-dimensional scenery.

**Flies** (or **Fly Loft**) – The space above a stage, where some lights and scenery are hung. The control of this area is in the hands of the **Flyman**, or better stated, **Fly Person.**

**Flop Sweat** – The perspiration – real or imagined – that covers your body (and your mind) when you're onstage and realize that you're doing a terrible job, and the audience has become restless, if not hostile.

**Footlights** (or **Foots**) – The downstage edge of the Apron, where recessed lighting was at one time housed, primarily to light the actors' faces from underneath, to add dimension – and, largely, to help erase the dewlaps, or wattles, or "cottage cheese" from the throats of aging performers.  They also created a theatrical spray of light on the closed Curtain, drawing the audience's anticipatory attention to the stage, shortly before the play began.

Older theatres may still have Foots, but they are rarely designed into new buildings.

Some directors will still use the term as an imaginary line, far Downstage: "Cross to the Foots, and then turn and speak to the mortician."

**Fourth Wall** – The imaginary wall filling the Proscenium Arch, so named because the scenery, whether a Box Set or open stage, is generally designed as three sides of a rectangle – with the remaining side, the Fourth Wall, being removed so the Audience can see what's going on.

The actors reinforce this convention by treating that "wall" as if it existed.

**Freeze** – Late in the rehearsal period, when the structure of the performance seems exactly right, the director will declare the play "Frozen," after which no one will make any changes in the pattern. (Unless you have a great new idea approved by the director!)

AND: After a Laugh Line has been delivered, and "buttoned," everyone on stage "freezes," silently, to allow the audience to laugh without missing any of the plot.

**Front of House** – The lobby, box office, restrooms, offices, coat-check room, etc.

**George Spelvin** – A traditional *nom de theatre* used when an actor doesn't want to be listed in the program, or when the same actor is playing several roles. There have been many Georgina Spelvins throughout history, too. (As with many theatre traditions, nobody really knows how this one began.)

**Ghost** – A theatre ghost is a wonderful asset to any backstage, and any production, for such spirits are almost always friendly, having been actors themselves. Even people who don't believe in ghosts have reported feeling positive and supportive energy off in the wings and the dark corners of the Stage House.

**Go Up** – To lose your lines. (See also "**Dry**".)

In a happier sense, it also means the Opening Curtain, which, we hope, "goes up" at the advertised time.

**Green Room** – A backstage area where cast and crew may relax when they're not needed on stage.  It's often also the place where the audience meets the actors after the performance.

**"Grocery List"** - The derogatory name given to the rote reading of a speech, without emotion or careful phrasing.

**Half-Hour** – Formally, "a half-hour before the curtain goes up," when in professional theatre the actors must arrive and check in. See **Call Time**.

**Ham acting** – overplaying, vocally, physically, and/or emotionally. A no-no.

**House** – The Auditorium, in which the audience sits to watch the play.

**House Lights** – The bright lights illuminating the Auditorium. The timing of when these are turned on or off during a performance, and whether they're faded slowly or rapidly, or just Snapped, is another tool at the director's disposal, for setting the key to the production's mood and style.

**Illusion of the First Time** – No matter how many times an actor has said a line or performed an action, in rehearsal and in previous performances, it seems to the audience that they're witnessing it fresh and new.  This should be the goal of every actor for every moment on stage.

**Image** – The personal picture, or sound, created in the actor's mind, or gut, that helps project to the audience that which does not exist; e.g. a voice on the telephone, or an automobile pulling up outside the window, or the taste of sirloin steak when it's merely a piece of toast cut to look like meat, etc.

**Imagery** – The figurative language used by poetic playwrights to evoke emotional responses in the audience, consciously or subconsciously.

**Improvisation (**or **"Improv")** – Working without a script. In rehearsal, or acting class, creating a scene alone or with other actors, and just the bare bones of a situation, can help you get in touch with emotions, or free your inhibitions. Many theatre companies present entire performances (usually comic) of Improvs, often building on a few key words suggested by the audience.

**Indicating** – A deadly sin on stage. Externally "pretending" to experience that which does not exist; e.g., "Owwwwww!! My head aches so much!!" – or – Bulging out your eyes when the person your character loves enters the stage. – or - Flaring your nostrils when the person your character hates enters the stage. Pointedly wiping your brow, to show how hot it is supposed to be, falls into this prohibited category, as does leaving your shirttail hanging out after an offstage fight.    (See **Mugging**.)

**Instrument** – A not-so-fanciful way of referring to your body and your voice, for they are to your artistic presentation as a violin or piano is to a musician.
        And Stage Lights are referred to as "Instruments."

**Intermission** – Break Time between the acts, when the audience can stretch their legs and chat about the play, and you can towel off, check your make-up, change your costume, and catch your breath. This is often the time the stage crew changes the set, so the next act opens in a new location. Generally 10 or 15 minutes long.

**Laugh Line** – Just as its name implies, it's a line of dialogue that should (but doesn't always) make the audience laugh.

**Left** - See **Stage Left**.

**Lightning Bolt** – The upward trajectory of the play, from the Opening Curtain to the Final Line of dialogue.

**Line** – A sentence from the script, or an entire long speech, that makes up your continuous dialogue at a single time.

   (And, when you begin rehearsing Off Book and forget your next few words, you call "Line!" and the Stage Manager provides it.)

**Magic Triangle** – The area of your body through which much of your emotion is projected, second only in importance to your face. The Triangle contains the space created by an imaginary line connecting your shoulders and descending from one shoulder to your belly button, then rising back up to the other.

**Melpomene** – The Muse of Tragedy.  (See **Thalia**)

**Milking It** - Another crime that actors must stay away from, in both comedy and drama.  Squeezing every drop of pathos as you elongate a death scene, or broadening your grin to the point of breaking your face after delivering a laugh line too loudly and too broadly.  Avoid.

**Miss Galflong** – An imaginary, outdated teacher of "elocution," whose rules of stage deportment are referenced in this book as What NOT to Do in Today's Theatre.

The **Moment** – In the play, each single successive unit of, not just Time, but also Emotion, Character, Plot, and Blocking.  When you're asked to "Play the moment," it means to shut out the rest of the world, and concentrate all of you on that specific instant. Perhaps it's a turning point, or just a simple line of dialogue, where the director feels your attention is wandering and your energy flagging.

**Monologue** – One character's long continuous speech.  In a classical play, it's called a Soliloquy.

**Mugging** – Making a face, avoiding inner truth by trying externally to show happiness, anger, etc.  This is Indicating of the worst sort.

**Narrow Base** – Standing with the feet very close together.  It weakens the look of your character, and in fact makes you look as if you could be tipped over by a touch, or even a loud voice, so it should be used sparingly, if at all.

**Off Book** – When you've memorized your lines for a certain portion of the play, which has been Blocked and Worked, and now you've laid aside your script.  The director will advise you that "Next Tuesday's rehearsal will be Act I, off book," which means: "It's time, or past time, to learn the lines!"

**Offstage** – Out of the audience's view, behind the Set, or in the Wings, but usually close by, so you can be heard if you have dialogue to toss in.

**Onstage** – Within sight of the audience, and therefore In Character and projecting Actor's Energy.

**Open** – Positioning yourself so most of your face, and most of your torso (the Magic Triangle), is fully visible to the audience.

**Orchestra Pit** – The big cavity in the floor, usually rectangular, which in many theatres separates the Stage from the House, in which an orchestra plays during a musical.  When not housing musicians it is also frequently used as part of the action (a swimming pool, a trench in wartime, a passage to a lower floor) – or can be covered over to extend the Apron, and thus the acting area, closer to the Audience.

**Outside Ear** – Your own careful attention to what you Sound Like at every moment on stage, similar to the Outside Eye.

**Outside Eye** – Checking your appearance onstage, as if you could actually see, externally, what every part of your body looks like to the audience. A necessary attribute to develop.

**Pace** – The rate of speech and movement on stage. Faster for a Comedy, more measured for a Drama – but always more intense and of greater urgency than your offstage everyday speed.

**Part** – The character whom you've been Cast to play. (Also called the Role)

**Pattern** – The consistent structure of the play, and thus of your role, achieved and "frozen" through successive rehearsals, which allows you to recreate the same performance, night after night.

**Performance** – Presenting the rehearsed play for the Audience.

**Period Play** – A plot set in the past, requiring costumes and movements of that period of history.

**"Phoning it in"** – Another onstage sin, meaning that you're only going through the motions onstage, with your concentration and focus elsewhere, perhaps on what you're going to have for dinner after the show, or who in the audience possesses that sweet girlish laugh. This can happen when a play has run for even a few weeks, and it must be anticipated and forestalled.

**"Places"** - The Call by the Stage Manager before each Act of the play, to bring the actors to where they begin the Act, on or off stage.

**Platform** – A raised portion of the stage scenery, providing variety in the height of acting areas, as stairs, alcoves, balconies, etc, and of the actors who stand on them.

**Play** – A literary work written for the Theatre, and the performance of that work before a live audience.

## Playbook – See Script

**Playwright** – The man or woman who sat in front of a blank sheet of paper and created the original work of art for us to perform. This person is Not called a "Playwrite," because plays are not Written, they are Wrought!!

**Plot** – The story of the play. A typical Plot has a recognizable beginning, middle, and end.

**Prepare** - Far more than being an everyday verb in the English language, meaning "To make ready," 'Prepare' in theatre jargon mandates **your vital duty as an actor before every entrance in every performance**, to warm up your voice and your body, and to check to be sure that you're equipped with your complete costume, your props, your first emotion and your first line.

**Producer** – Usually the Big Boss, but different theatres assign the title differently. This high-ranking person may raise the money to present the play, hire everybody from the director on down, and sign all the paychecks; or may be responsible solely for the technical departments, or serve in whatever way the job has evolved over the years in a particular group.

**Production** – A theatrical work (usually a play or a musical) presented for an audience.

**Projection** – Sending your voice strongly into every area of the House.
      It is also a method of creating two-dimensional scenery or visible atmospheric moods.

**Prompt** – To provide a word, or several, to an actor in rehearsal who's forgotten what comes next and calls: "Line!" It's usually the Stage Manager who tosses in the needed dialogue, or someone called, logically enough, the Prompter. Most theatres have thankfully abandoned the practice of having a Prompter whispering lines to actors during <u>performances</u>, because knowing that help is at hand could create laziness in an actor who was so inclined; and it sadly notifies the audience that something's amiss.

**<u>Props</u>** – (formally "**Properties**") – Everything that is found on stage, except actors. Books, bottles, guns, flowers, food, etcetc. In some theatres, furniture is under the control of the Prop Crew. In a particular outdoor production of "A Midsummer Night's Dream," live horses were under the control of Props.

**<u>Proscenium arch</u>** – The "picture frame" opening that separates the auditorium (the House) from the Stage, and directly behind which the Stage Curtain hangs.

**<u>Proscenium Stage</u>** – The platform at one end of a room, on which the Set is set behind the Curtain and the Proscenium Arch. In the mid-20th century, most stages in the Western world were Prosceniums, but since then Arenas and Thrusts have become far more common, as have other configurations and juxtapositions of audience-and-actor.

**<u>Prototype</u>** – A real person whom an actor calls to mind to help create a Character close to the role as written, but different in movement, vocal quality, temperament, etc, from the actor.

**<u>Rehearse/Rehearsal</u>** – To prepare the play for performance, as led by the director.

**<u>Rhythm/Tempo</u>** – Tools to help an actor create a specific character:

      **<u>Rhythm</u>** is the <u>overall</u> motion of your character's Voice and Body <u>throughout the play</u> (Slow, Fast, Lumbering, Twinkling, etc.)

      And **<u>Tempo</u>** is each <u>moment-by-moment</u> change of pace (loving, angry, fearful, et al.) WITHIN that Rhythm.

**<u>Right</u>** - See **<u>Stage Right</u>**.

**<u>Role</u>** - See <u>Part</u>

**<u>Run</u>** – The length of time by the <u>clock</u> the production takes. ("We ran 10 minutes long last night.")  AND: The length of time by the <u>calendar</u> the production takes ("We usually run two weekends, but the crowds have been so big we've added an extra performance.")

**<u>Run-through</u>** (or **<u>Runthru</u>**) – In rehearsal, going straight through a scene, or an act, without stopping.  This helps you see which of your moments need work, and how better to pace your emotional builds and your output of energy.  It helps the director see how well the entire fabric of the play is coalescing – or not.

**<u>Scenery</u>** - See **Set.**

**<u>Script</u>** (also called the Playbook) - The printed text of the play, into which the actor will write personal blocking, emotional and line notes, and the Stage Manager will insert into the Master Script the blocking for every character, as well as all Light Cues, Sound Cues, etc.  Use a pencil, please, for any of this may change, frequently, during the days or weeks of rehearsal.

**<u>Selectivity</u>** – When faced with an almost infinite number of choices and decisions (gestures, crosses, tempi, emotions, tones of voice, etc) for practically every one of your lines, Selectivity is your own artistic discrimination that allows you (or forces you) to choose the single correct one each time.  Or maybe the next time.

**<u>Set</u>** (or **<u>Setting</u>**) – the scenery which represents the location where the play takes place, amid which, or in front of which, the actors do their stuff.

**<u>Shock of Recognition</u>** – Causing audience members to see themselves, through a line of dialogue, an action or behavioral pattern in a character, or a plot turn in the performance.

**Sight lines** (often spelled **"Site" lines**) – Imaginary straight lines stretching from the extreme seats in the House, both far left and far right, past the Proscenium Arch to the farthest Up Stage point, to make clear to the set designer, the director and the actors the limits on Stage Right and Stage Left beyond which some of the audience can't see all the action.  If you want to remain in view, keep Onstage of the Sight Lines.

**Slapstick** – A comedy device, comprising two flat slats of wood, attached at one end, which, when smacked by a comic actor against another's bottom, makes a satisfying Slap noise, louder and safer – and funnier - than thwacking that same bottom with a single board! Though the slapstick itself isn't used very much any more, its name has been applied to knockabout Farce comedy, such as The Three Stooges, and plays like "Lend Me a Tenor" and "Noises Off."

**Sotto Voce** – Speaking in an undertone, a whisper, so another character (supposedly) can't hear you - - but with enough Support so the Audience CAN.

**Speech** – Several lines of dialogue, often a paragraph, spoken by one actor, forming a single Thought Group. This "Speech" isn't that which you find in a lecture hall or on a politician's platform, and it's usually funnier or more dramatic than either of those – and is longer than a single line in the script.

**Specificity** - Distinct details of your performance, adding to its believability and to the audience's interest in it, and you.

**Stage** – The area on which the action of the play takes place.  It may be a Proscenium, Arena, or Thrust Stage, or any other designated space, set aside for the performance.

**Stage Crew** – Taking their cues from the Stage Manager, this backstage staff is in charge of sound and lighting cues, costume changes, raising and lowering the Curtain, placement of props and furniture, and the mounting and moving of scenery.

**Stage Door** – Access for the cast and crew into the backstage area, without going through the front-of-house areas, visible to the audience.

**Stage Fright** – A fear that can attack an actor, causing him to believe that he's unable to perform, and often causing him to "dry", or "go up," driving his lines right out of his memory.  Many famous and talented artists have been beset with this frightening malady, sometimes for years.  Its scientific names are *topophobia* and *glossophobia,* but we don't need Greek or Latin for its cure, which simply is: "You're a human being, too strong and too wise to succumb to a mindless fear.  You can defeat it!!"

**Stage Left** – The left side of the stage, from the actor's point of view facing into the House.

**Stage House** – The entire enclosure that contains the stage, the wings, the flies, and the pipes holding the onstage lighting instruments.

**Stage Manager** – The director's right-hand person, who organizes rehearsals, records all the blocking, and, when the show moves into Dress Rehearsal and performance, takes charge of the whole operation, cuing the Actors and Crews, starting the play at the advertised time, and, throughout the days or weeks of the run of the show, maintains the smoothness of the performances and backstage discipline, exactly as the director determined.   (Abbreviated "SM".)

**Stage Presence** – The assurance that you'll bring to the audience when your talent, your belief in your readiness in this role, and your actor's energy are spilling by the bucketful out of every pore.  And if you aren't actually so assured, then you'd better Act as if you were.

**Stage Right** - The right side of the stage, from the actor's point of view facing into the House.

**Standard Speech** – The neutral, natural middle-American dialect that audiences from any part of the country can easily understand.

**<u>Standing Ovation</u>** – (or **"<u>Standing O</u>"**) - - During Curtain Calls, when most of the audience rise from their seats while applauding. As you can imagine, it's a wonderful tribute to the cast, and the entire production.  And you love it when it happens!!

**<u>Stanislavski, Konstantin Sergeyevich</u>** (1863-1938) – Founder of the Moscow Art Theatre, and developer of "The System" - an emotional approach to acting which, somewhat altered, came to the U.S. as "The Method," and is the basis for most of the acting styles in the Western world today.

**<u>Stealing Focus</u>** – deliberately or inadvertently bringing the audience's attention to you, when it should be on another actor. This could be caused by a sudden movement, or a noise like a cough or rattling ice in a glass.  Forbidden.  And not very polite.

**<u>Strike</u>** – Taking something (e.g. a Prop) off stage.  And, usually immediately after the closing performance, taking down the set.

**<u>Superstitions</u>** – Theatre people are often (or pretend to be) very superstitious, and therefore follow some archaic traditions, chief of which is the prohibition of quoting from, or even saying aloud the title of, the Scottish play ("Macb- -h") because of its history of accidents and even deaths.  Whistling in the dressing room is also frowned on, as is the use of peacock feathers onstage, and wishing anyone "Good Luck," lest it bring Bad Luck instead.  "Break a leg" is preferred, or, as translated from the German *Hals und Beinbruch*: "Neck and leg break."

**<u>Support</u>** – The conscious reinforcing of your voice, usually by breath control, to help propel your lines to all corners of the House.

**<u>Technical Rehearsal</u>** (Or "**<u>Tech</u>**") – Many theatres, after the scenery is fully built and painted and installed onstage, will schedule a Tech Rehearsal on the set for the Crew, before the first Dress Rehearsal, at which all the cues are run in sequence: front curtain up and down, lights, sound, scene changes, all technical aspects of the performance.  It's often conducted without the cast, but sometimes the actors will be asked to be there to go through their dialogue leading up to each technical cue, in what is called a "cue-to-cue" rehearsal. This may or may not have you in costume.

**Technique** – The craft and skills of an actor, encompassing all that is described in this book.

**Tempo** – The rate at which a character moves and speaks on stage. (See: **Rhythm/Tempo**)

**Thalia** – The Muse of Comedy.  (See **Melpomene**)

**Theatre** – The fine art to which everything in this book is dedicated.  And the building which contains it (From the Greek for "a place for seeing").

## Theatre-in-the-Round – see **Arena Theatre**.

**Thespian** – A 21st-century Actor, named for Thespis, the 6th-century B.C. Greek poet.
Also a secondary-school association of acting students.

**"They"** – The Audience, who are so important to what we do that this one-syllable pronoun stands for a whole theatre full of independent entities.   "How are They reacting tonight?"  "Did They get the Shakespeare joke?"  "They're restless.  I think They're worried about the snowstorm predicted in town."  Without consciously forgetting the word 'Audience,' even newcomers to the Theatre find themselves saying, "I hope They like the new blocking of the love song."

**Thought Group** – All the sentences and phrases in an actor's line of dialogue (or several consecutive lines) that center on a single subject. When the script brings that subject to an end, it's usually time for a Transition.

**Three-Build** – A useful tool for the actor, finding in the script a natural opportunity to build vocally or emotionally Upward (or

Downward) on three successive words or phrases; e.g. "You're a <u>rat</u>, a <u>skunk</u> and a <u>dirty dog</u>!"

**<u>Three-quarter position</u>** – Placing your feet in a modified T-shape while standing, which allows the audience to see your face and Magic Triangle, and hear your dialogue, while still keeping you realistically in contact with the other actors on stage. (Often expressed numerically, as "¾ position.")

**<u>Thrust Stage</u>** – Very much like Shakespeare's Globe Theatre, the audience is arranged on three sides of the stage, allowing just one wall – the upstage wall – for scenery, doors, windows, etc. Like an Arena Stage, it brings more of the audience closer to the action than the Proscenium Stage.

**<u>Tight Cue</u>** – Speaking <u>immediately</u> after you've received your cue from another actor. The ideal Tight Cue is achieved by saying your First Word at the exact same time that you're hearing the Last Word of the cue line. The audience's ears will sort it out, effortlessly, and they'll appreciate the thrilling onward pace of the show.

**<u>Transition</u>** – The graceful evolving from one emotion to another. The audience travels on Transitions, so if you don't find them, and create them, and present them, the audience won't be moving along with you through the performance. You'll have lost them.

**<u>Tryouts</u>** – See **Auditions.**

**<u>Understudy</u>** – An actor who has learned the lines and been rehearsed in a role, or several roles, in the play, in case one of the original actors is unable to perform. Sometimes an understudy never gets to go on at all, but some understudies have become famous when, having been called upon at the very last moment, have given beautiful performances – and been rewarded with a movie contract, or jewels and big cars and a line-up of handsome royalty waiting outside the Stage Door.

**Unity of Style** – The careful attention to detail to make sure that every aspect of the Production is of the same style: Comedy or Drama?  1920 or 2012?  Fantasy or Stark Realism?   Poetry or Prose?

**Upstage** – The portion of the Stage farthest away from the audience.

**Upstaging** – The dastardly practice of moving Upstage of another actor, forcing her to turn her face, and her voice, away from the audience in order to look at you.

**"Use it"** – If something goes wrong on stage that cannot be easily covered up - such as a large prop or a costume piece falling to the floor, or a door that won't open, or another actor failing to appear on cue - then you must incorporate it into the action; you must "use it."  Keep it in the style of the production, and the audience will understand, and appreciate your skill, especially if it's a comedy and you can solve the problem humorously.  But avoid Creating a problem, just to show how Well you use it.

The term also applies to allowing the glitch to feed your character's emotion at that moment.  If you're angry and the bottle won't open, "use it" to enhance your anger.  If you're sad and your dress rips, "use it."

**Variety** – This is what the British call Vaudeville.  And it's the name of the newspaper of show business, issued in both daily and weekly editions.  But mainly it's one of an actor's most important tools, to keep the vocal and physical aspects of your performance moving and changing, always interesting and magnetic.  Impose variety when necessary.

**Vector** – The invisible path of an actor's movement, usually to or from a doorway, a piece of furniture, or another actor.

**Volume** – See **Projection** and **Support**.

**<u>Walk-on</u>** – A role with no dialogue, often a member of a crowd scene.

**<u>Warm-Ups</u>** - Physical and vocal exercises an actor does before rehearsals and performances, sometimes alone and sometimes with the whole cast.

**<u>Wings</u>** – Unseen by the audience, these are the offstage spaces, Left and Right of the Set, where the actors and Stage Crew wait for their cues.

**<u>Working Rehearsal</u>** – After a scene has been Blocked, the next time it's rehearsed will be a Working Rehearsal, in which the director may adjust some of the Blocking, or add some more, as deficiencies or new ideas appear. The actors are usually still carrying their scripts at this rehearsal, and inserting any changes.

**<u>Work Lights</u>** – Usually bare white, very bright, stage lighting used for building the Sets, and for Rehearsals.

**"<u>Yip</u>"**- The supposedly "involuntary" sound you must make when, within the blocking, you're hit, or you hit someone else, or bump your elbow, or trip going up the stairs, etc. This might be an "ooof" or "uhhh" or "aaaaaah." Without hearing the Yip, the audience won't believe the moment, because when They crack Their elbows, They Yip.

# Chapter 2

# <u>SOME TRUTHS</u> and <u>MAXIMS OF THE</u> <u>THEATRE</u>, to start with

We theatre people make a bargain with each member of each audience that enters our auditorium:  If they will bring a **<u>Willing suspension of disbelief,</u>** we'll give them a wonderful theatrical experience.

Samuel Taylor Coleridge (author of  "The Rime of the Ancient Mariner") coined that 'Suspension of Disbelief' phrase in 1817, wonderfully challenging down through the years poets and playwrights – and us sweaty thespians – to be worthy of the trust those audiences give us.  They voluntarily agree to believe for a few hours that what they see on stage really is a living room or a blasted heath or the deck of a ship, and that the people appearing in those locations for some reason all face outward when they talk, and that cute young couple truly falls in love, and that evil landlord dies right there alone in the spotlight.

And the simple exchange that we give for their trust in us is to present to them these characters, these emotions, these ideas, these stories, <u>as skillfully as we can</u>.

If we are ill-prepared (whether in the scene shop or the rehearsal room), or if we only bring a half-concentration onto the stage, or if we resent or regret the material of the play and thereby offer it mealy-mouthed – then we are failing in our obligations to an audience who has committed itself, individually and collectively, to sit still and watch us and listen to us for the length of the presentation. (And, not incidentally, those folks have probably laid out some dollars in order to do so).

This small book offers a number of thoughts toward achieving those skills that nightly help us earn their willingly suspending their disbelief.

\*

### Every work of art is a new look at the human condition.

Theatre Art, involving as it does living actors occupying the same space and breathing the same air as their patrons, is an Immediate, Right-Now look at humanity.

To that end, each rehearsal and each performance should be a New new look at the people who share our world, and not just a repetition of yesterday's performance.

\*

**Business. Business. Business.** If talking heads on television are boring (and they usually are) then static, unmoving Bodies on stage are worse. **Do something**!

The word **"Acting,"** from the Latin "actus" **means just that**: **"Doing."**

Grab a prop and use it to help manifest your character and emotions, and you'll carry the audience with you as you Do things, not so much when you stand and deliver long-winded proclamations.  Yes, even in a Greek tragedy or a Shakespeare history.

This is Theatre, not Radio.

\*

### Each of us in the theatre serves Two bosses.

If actors were asked: "For whom are you performing this play?" many would reply, "The Director," or "The Producer," or, half-jokingly, "My paycheck."  And, sure, there's validity in each of those answers.  But I urge that, instead, you seriously consider the fact that **the Playwright and the Audience are in fact our chief motivators.**

**THE PLAYWRIGHT** merits the very best work we can give to this one true creative Theatre Artist, who sat down with a blank sheet of paper, and from raw guts, spirited imagination, heightened sensitivity, and technique with words, characterizations, plotting, scene structure and the Lightning Bolt - out of a deep knowledge of and feeling for people - has created the initial Work of Theatre Art – **the Play.  The Script.**

The rest of us, actors, directors, designers, et al, are Re-Creative artists.  Oh, Yes, I hope that we are Creative, too - - but we are fortunate enough to have an already-existing Work of Art in our hands from the very first day, that Script which the Playwright has given us, and from which we will (re)create a New work of Art called The Production.

(I'm not discounting Improvisational Theatre, or theatre in which the script is created by the entire company.  But these art forms occupy a very small percentage of theatre today, around the world.)

Then: the production of a play isn't complete until the Final Actor has arrived – **THE AUDIENCE –** our second and equally important Motivator.  Audience reactions, positive and negative, their understanding of what we're doing, their sensitivities toward every line, every movement, should now affect the timing of the whole performance.

These people have traveled from their homes and sat themselves down in our building, our space, and in exchange for our performance are giving us something very precious as their Ticket of Admission.  And it's Not their Cash.

It's their Time.  It's Themselves, that they're unqualifiedly offering to us; their Attention, and, one hopes, their Emotions.  They're trusting us with all of this, so surely we owe them, in return, Every Bit of Ourselves, all our talents, the depths of our feelings and the breadth of our intellects, all our rehearsed moments, with which we'll present to them the work of our first Motivator, the Playwright.

*

An old circus proverb says that **The thrill is gone if we see perspiration on the tightrope-walker's face**.  Oh, Yes, we must realize that it's terribly difficult up there, and that the performer is supremely focused, and could certainly fail – and fall – but we must also know that she wouldn't be on that wire if she couldn't perfectly perform her stunts for a tentful of breathless fans.  We're frightened, but at the same time reassured.

It's true in the theatre, too.  If the audience sees you fumbling for lines, hiding behind another actor, beginning the song on a wrong note, they are in truth "seeing the perspiration," and that's not why they came.  Involve them in the Character's problems and challenges, Not the actor's.  Show them that the actor is well under control.

If you really don't know what you're doing, and the perspiration is Real, the name for that is "Flop Sweat," which can easily be avoided by your hard work through all the rehearsals, and all the performances.

*

I always cringe when an audience member says of an actor's work in a play:  "Oh, she's just like my next door neighbor."   NO!  Please – No!  If the public wants total verisimilitude, and photographic reproductions of familiar figures, please guide them to the nearest movie multiplex.  <u>**Characters on stage, though based on life, must be BIGGER THAN LIFE**</u>.

The theatre began at the foot of a Greek hill, in plays featuring only gods and heroes, with emotions of such gigantic stature that, as they metamorphosed into human speech, they were hurled at the audiences through megaphones built into the masks the actors wore.
OK, we've allowed common folk like you and me onto the stage for a long time now, but we retain the legacy of strong vocal projection, and deeply-felt emotions, and plots dealing with vital issues and searing conflicts.

We have in today's theatre many fine "kitchen-sink" and naturalistic plays with scenery so real that a child in the audience will cry out, "I want to go play in that garden," as one supposedly shouted when "The Seagull" was first produced in Moscow in 1898, featuring three-dimensional sets, and forever altering and improving our theatre arts.

But you, the actor of today, must not be seduced by this solid scenery, or lamps that light or spigots that pour forth water, or by the "real folks" dialogue you're given to speak, into playing your role so REAL that neither your words nor your facial expressions nor your bodily movements communicate beyond the first row.

Yes, <u>what we do is BASED on real people in real situations,</u> but the ideas and emotions of a play are projected to the audience using acting techniques which keep the reality, but give it a boost up into Theatrical Realism, which will grab the audience in Row A and Row L and Row ZZ, and hold them throughout the evening – which couldn't happen if all the vocal and emotional projection, and the level of Actor's Energy, were pulled back to the meat-and-potatoes of Photographic Realism.  Save it for when a camera and a microphone are three inches from your face, and thus the audience seemingly just as close.

A day in my life, or yours, I'd bet, presented on stage, would be horribly dull.

One technique to help present a deeper and more intense Stage Life is to set a goal for yourself of reaching, in every rehearsal, for **<u>Higher Highs and Lower Lows.</u>**

Plumb the Depths, and Scale the Heights - of emotion, of the volume of your projected voice, of energy, of laugh lines, of filling meaningful pauses.

Push the limits at both ends, and never hold back, but trust your director to rein you in if you go too far in rehearsal.  Throw Yourself into the Role - deepening your emotions, strengthening your voice, finding all the facets of your character, sharpening your comic timing, striving with all of your instruments to be more stageworthy (which means of course: "Worthy of being on this stage!")

When the director tamps you down a little, you should be pleased, for that means that you've broken through the imaginary line of caution that inhibits too many actors.  With that kind of sharp attention from the director, you'll find the perfect limits, high and low, by Final Dress Rehearsal.  At that time, or shortly before, the director will Freeze the performance.  No more experimenting when you're that close to meeting the audience.

Just maintain in every performance those High Highs, and Low Lows, to the best levels of your best rehearsal.

*

What can you - as an actor - do to help **illuminate the Title of the Play**?

The best playwrights agonize over what to call their creations, because the title explains the play in brief, and forever afterward that plot and those characters will be identified in an instant by the title, on a poster, a program, and the cover of the script, and part of your duty as a member of the cast is to contribute to bringing that title to life.

After you're off-book, it's a good idea in the rehearsal room to leave your script on a chair near the acting area, with the title always visible as you rehearse, to remind you of the ultimate decision the playwright made – The Name of the Play - so you can contribute in even the smallest way to make that title live.

In "Twelfth Night," for example, you should bring a festive atmosphere to each moment you're on stage, remembering that twelve nights after December 25th is Epiphany, when much of the world joyously celebrates Christmas.

In "Guys and Dolls," keep in mind always that the title is not "Men and Women" or "Boys and Girls."  You've got to play a Guy or a Doll, because the playwright has given you unmistakable titular instructions toward your musical comic characterization.

With the title, "The Crucible," Arthur Miller has told you what blazing environment surrounds the town of Salem, the people, their religion, and their government.  So each actor must always move within that crucible, being subjected to impossibly high strictures, and tightly-focused, mostly unreasonable, tests of character.

The audience knew the title of the play they bought tickets for, and the programs in their laps reinforce that title . . . . and so must you.

*

**The audience sees everything**.  So: **Always Be Specific**, in all you do on stage.

If you're weeping, be sure your sorrowful shoulders are visible to the audience, even if your face is not.

If you're writing a letter, actually Write Something – not just scribbles; and if you're saying aloud the words while you're writing, be sure that five words of speech are balanced by five words on the page – not three or twelve.

If you're pouring a drink or a cup of coffee, fill the receptacle at least three-quarters full.  Some theatres insist on just an inch of liquid, fearing that you'll spill any more.  Good grief!  Trust your hands not to slop your liquids, and let the audience see that you're really pouring just as they do at home.

Even if you're only a walk-on, one small part of a huge crowd scene, some of the audience will let their eyes rest on you for a few seconds, so let them know that you're absolutely part of that event, as they see you clearly reacting to the stimulus being thrown at you, whether it's a doomed man mounting the scaffold, or a weaselly congressman answering questions, or Mary Poppins rising to the ceiling of the theatre.

They see everything, so let them see specificity in all things.

*

**The "Lightning Bolt" is the trajectory of the play**, from Opening Curtain to Final Blackout, as intensity begins and grows, and lessens, and grows again, up and up throughout the performance.

The director, of course, is responsible for determining the Lightning Bolt of the entire play, but within that overall upward thrust you have **your own Lightning Bolt** (see Figure 1), which you must create during rehearsals, and which will guide you through your performance, and pull the audience along with you – on your trajectory from your first entrance to the last time we see you on stage before the Curtain Call.

Your first entrance (or if you're discovered on stage when the curtain opens) is of course when the Lightning Bolt of your character begins, and starts climbing upward, communicating your intensity and energy to the audience.  And <u>never again will that energy drop as low as at its beginning</u>.

As your Lightning Bolt moves **upward** through the performance, there will be of necessity occasional slightly **downward** diversions, because <u>to move continually upwards</u> in tension until the end of the play, with no escape hatches, (as in Figure 2) <u>would cause the audience's heads to explode</u>.  And that would lessen their enjoyment of the play.

These <u>necessary **downward diversions,**</u> these gentle relaxations, are created by laughs, by entrances of new characters, by scene breaks or intermissions, and by your transitions into less-intense emotions.

<u>This is true whether the play is a comedy or a drama</u>, or an amalgam of both.

**Follow along on <u>Figure 1</u>, starting at the bottom of the page**.  It shows a single character's Lightning Bolt, following a plot line from an imaginary play, which we can call "Lightning Strikes Once," with Act I set in the kitchen of the house where your character, a divorced woman of  35, lives with her two young children.   There's a party going on, off stage.

- You enter the kitchen, and your **<u>Lightning Bolt starts, at its Lowest Level,</u>** with your stage presence and energy at a comparatively low intensity.  It's of course already higher than was the audience's when they were chatting in the lobby, so you immediately grab their attention, and invite them to travel with you; you know absolutely that never again, throughout the play, will your energy and focus be at this lowest, beginning level.

Curtain Closes on Act I.

Gunshot.

You're VERY angry.

Marvin chastises you.

This makes you very angry.

Sally asks Marvin to drive her home.

Friend (Sally) intervenes,
calms things.
Most guests leave.

Children exit; argument recommences.

The children enter,
to say 'Good-Night.'

Intense argument; partygoers uncomfortable.

Your former sweetheart, Doug, denounces you.

Happy partygoers enter.
You join in the gaiety.

You kiss (Starting a new sort of tension).

You prove your
innocence.

Revelation of crime in your past.

Phone call, for Marvin. He watches you throughout.

Big laugh, generated
by the silly cook.

Conflict with Marvin.

Entrance of Marvin,
your boyfriend.

Exposition as you & cook prepare canapés, talk about the party in progress.

Your first entrance.

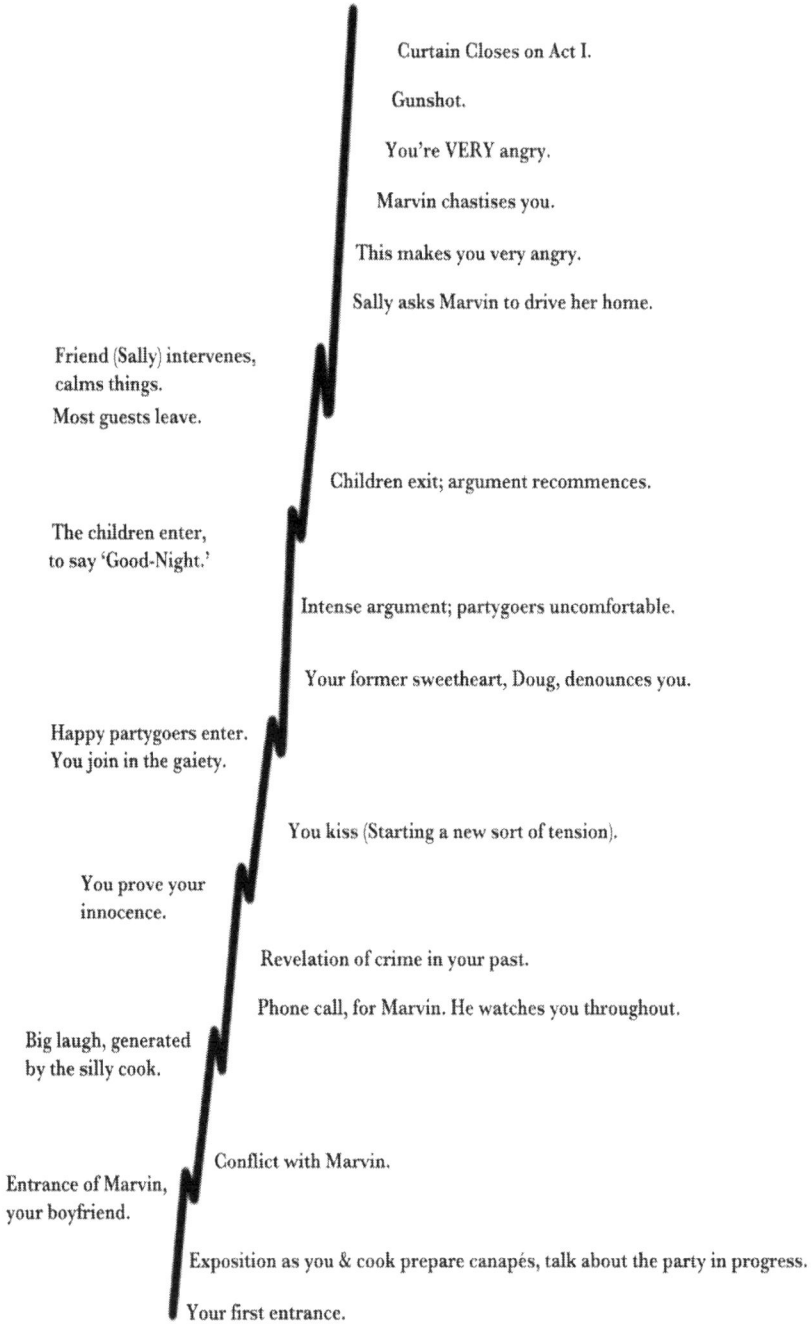

Figure 1. **The proper flow of the Lightning Bolt.**

- The Lightning Bolt immediately starts climbing, tightening your intensity slowly, as you and your cook discuss the people at the party, and a worry you have about a possibly very unpleasant situation - all of which is Exposition, telling the audience the beginnings of the Plot. We learn about you, and some of your likes and dislikes.

- Marvin, your boyfriend, enters. And, as usually happens in the early moments of any Act I, new characters enter for the audience to focus on and learn about **[More Exposition!],** and in this play you're glad Marvin's here, because you love him. You smile and relax a little. This gives you a respite from the upward climb of the Bolt, as you'll see in the slightly **downward diversion** in Figure 1, on Marvin's entrance.

- But Marvin speaks of some worries he has about you, and the Bolt turns right around and **starts back Up again**. Conflict (the major fuel that powers all good plots) erupts between you.

- The cook has been trying to make herself invisible over by the pantry door, but finally has to come forward into the middle of your argument. She utters a very silly, funny line with a big bowl of apples in her hands, and gets a robust laugh from the audience, which again grants you a **slightly downward diversion**, lightening the atmosphere a little.

- Marvin's cell phone rings. He takes it, but covers his conversation with his hand – and never takes his eyes off you. This tension starts the **Bolt back up again**. When the call is over, Marvin confronts you with an accusation of some major transgression you committed long ago. This continues to drive the **Bolt up, and up some more**.

*(As you follow this scenario along Figure 1, remember that this is YOUR personal Lightning Bolt. At many times, it may parallel the Play's Lightning Bolt, but you should not be concerned with anything at this point but your own **Rising Action**, and its occasional dip back into a **diversion**.)*

- With great sincerity and irrefutable facts, you <u>convince </u>Marvin that you're innocent. You both then relax a little, **creating a new downward diversion**. Then you kiss.

- Oh, boy! That kiss, beginning <u>within the downward diversion</u> of your Lightning Bolt, propels you right back <u>onto its upward track</u>, because, rather than relaxing you, the kiss of course introduces a different sort of tension – joy - into your somewhat-rocky relationship.

OK, I don't think we need to go on up through the entire Lightning Bolt of Figure 1 together, but I hope you'll continue now to follow the path we've started, to really understand how it can give you a strong and useful matrix with which and on which to structure your performance.

Notice how all the stimuli that create downward Diversions are written to the Left of the Bolt, adjacent to the **dips** that represent them, and the major stimuli that propel the Bolt **upward,** from your First Moment, are listed on the Right.

<u>Note especially</u> that:

- after you're first seen by the audience, your Lightning Bolt NEVER returns to that Lowest Level of Energy and Intensity Again. (<u>See Figure 3</u>)
- no downward Diversion EVER dips back even as far as the <u>previous segment</u> of your Bolt. Each is a minor dip, but the Bolt maintains your ever-upward journey.
- the last part of your Act I has <u>No downward Diversions</u>, as the Bolt is building, building, building, always upwards to the Curtain.

When you're first seen in <u>Act II</u> (not illustrated here), your Lightning Bolt need not start as high as Act I <u>ended</u>, but it <u>must not begin too many segments lower</u> than the last time you were seen.  And from then, of course, it'll start ever upward, building from there, with the same sort of respites, downward diversions, as were with you in Act I.

If there's an Act III (or IV in an O'Neill play, or V in a Shakespearean play) the successive shafts on your Lightning Bolt will be fashioned in the same way, beginning perhaps a bit lower than the last time you appeared, but never as low again as when you first entered, and moving thereafter up and up, with very necessary occasional relaxed moments in the slight downward dips of diversions.

This final act will of course be building toward the Climax of the play, which might also be the Climax of your character – the highest point on your Lightning Bolt.

\*

Can your Lightning Bolt grow and change during Rehearsals?  Oh, Yes; oh, Yes!  It Should . . . . as you and the director and the rest of the cast find new meanings and nuances and thrusts and dips in your production of the play.

Another excellent use of your Lightning Bolt in rehearsals is to help place each scene on the Bolt, so when you start to rehearse a scene beginning on Page 35, for example, you know just what level of intensity your character has reached by that point in the play - - and you won't make the common mistake of starting the scene with energy and intensity at the Page One lowest level.

\*

**YOUR FINAL EXIT IN ACT III**

**YOUR FIRST ENTRANCE**

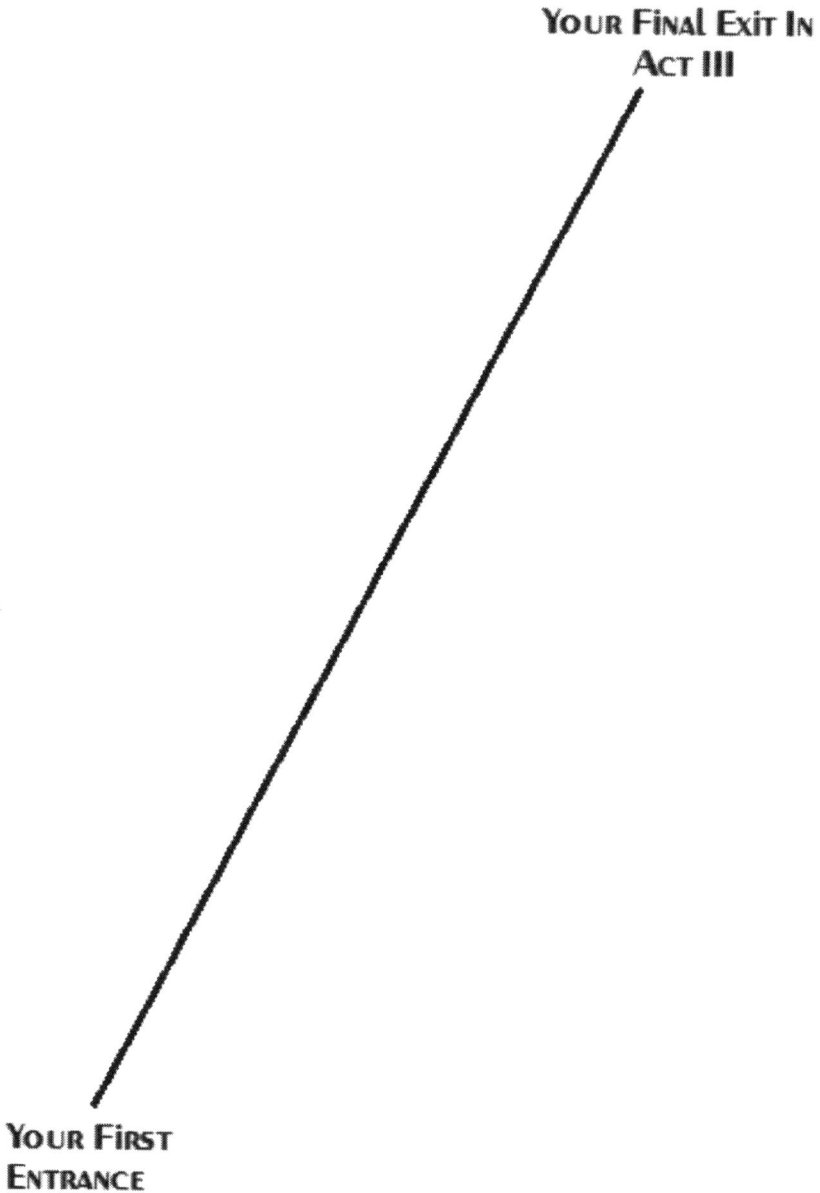

Figure 2. **A very WRONG Lightning Bolt, showing no relaxations.** This unrelieved upward thrust, with **no downward diversions** from your first moment to your last, would send you screaming out into the night, with the audience close behind you.

### <u>Think of your relationship with the audience as a Courtship</u>,
with your Lightning Bolt as the itinerary of your dating progress:

You meet, and go out for the first time.  You have dinner, and go to a movie.

A week later, you have another date.  Dinner and a movie.

A few days later, you get together again, and go out for dinner and see a movie.

A month later, you're back together, and have dinner and go to a movie.

Where is this very dull relationship going?  The audience, watching a play with this same sort of repetitiveness of anticipation/disappointment, wonders where the <u>play</u> is going.

It's represented by the dull sameness of <u>Figure 3</u>.  Your courtship can't sustain such a predictable, going-nowhere, uniformity, and neither can your Lightning Bolt.

*

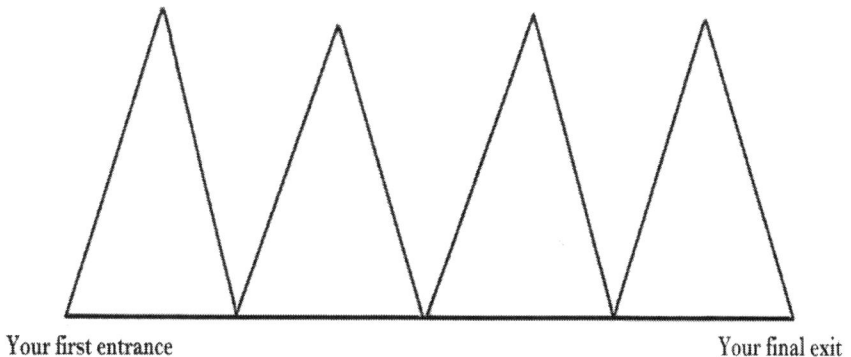

**Your first entrance**                              **Your final exit**

Figure 3.  **Another wrong Lightning Bolt,** showing **downward diversions** coming all the way back down to the level of intensity with which you began the play, and then having to build back up from your first appearance again and again.  **No diversion** should ever bring you back down even to the level of the previous segment of your Bolt, and certainly not back to the beginning.

**Fill Every Pause**.  Playwrights from Chekhov to Mamet have used pauses almost as dialog, causing what is Not said to be as important as, or more so than, actual sentences.  So please intensify your emotion, crank up your Actor's Energy, and Fill each pause a playwright (or director) calls for.  Three actors standing idly, emptily, staring at one another in silence, with no understanding why the author has left them hanging, will both bore and confuse your audience – and those aren't the verbs you want to generate.

\*

### "Theatre" or "Theater"?

Most people in this profession spell it with an "re" at the end.  "Theatre."

Most newspapers spell it with an "er."  "Theater."

In England, nearly everyone spells it "Theatre," which is why some American doubters think it's snooty or affected of us to spell it that way.

Sometimes a cinema is called a "Theater," while live actors work in a "Theatre."

An old actor told me that he believed the difference is that the Building was a "Theater," but the Art presented inside it was "Theatre."

However you choose to spell this age-old name of our art, please honor it with your best work.

\*

We're not always taken as seriously as we'd like, because **the product of all our rehearsals and long hours of creativity is called a "play**."  Like children in a sandbox.

Book, Painting, Symphony, Building, Statue – these terms have weight and substance, far more than "Play."

"Opus" means "<u>A Work</u>" and its plural, "Opera," means "<u>Works</u>." A strong affirmation of good hard labor, on behalf of the audience. Work! Works!! Not a thin little purposeless kiddie-pool word like "Play."

This historic misnomer has to spur us to make every production of every Play we present as skillful as we can, to rid that word of its vestige of lightweight fun and games, so even our sauciest comedies and wispiest musicals will be appreciated as well-done works of Art, as much so as any Opus.

Remember, too, that **Theatre includes Every Other Art**: Music, Dance, Literature, Poetry, Painting, Sculpture, Design, and Architecture. These artists, as we actors and directors, are always seeking new ways of examining and presenting the human condition. What a beautiful experience is given us, creating in concert with so many other artistic people to produce a Play! The word already sounds more substantial.

*

<u>Prepare</u>.  This is one of the most important duties you have as an actor, <u>before every entrance in every performance</u>.

Too many actors pride themselves on being able to tell a joke to their buddies offstage immediately before entering as the tragic King Lear, or Antigone defying her uncle. And that's too bad; they're cheating the audiences, and the other cast members, and Themselves, of something meaningful by demeaning their work, their art, as something to be disdained by giving it only minimal focus, almost as if they're embarrassed to take it seriously.

I recommend just the opposite: I strongly urge that, beginning ten minutes or so prior to each entrance, you get away from everyone else backstage, and **<u>Prepare</u>**:

Double-check to be sure that your costume is complete, and that you have all the props that should be in your pocket or in your hands for the upcoming scene.

Further, Prepare your<u>self</u> . . .

. . . by pulling the first line of dialogue out of your memory bank and laying it carefully across your tongue;
. . . by assuming upon yourself the person that you're playing, reminding your body of the physical traits, and your mind and heart of the inner life of your character;
. . . by revivifying the first emotion of your scene;
. . . by loosening your body (your instrument) with stretches, and your voice with big yawns;
. . . by shaking your wrists wildly, eliminating tension, generating actor's energy;
. . . and (sounding silly, but deadly serious) if your knees tend to crack, do some knee-bends, so they crack only Offstage.

No, with all this **Preparation** to be done, there's no time and no excuse for joking and chatting right up to your first moment.

A famous actor playing the lead in a long-run Broadway musical was said to put on his make-up and his first costume in his apartment, and arrive at the theatre in a taxi, just in time to come in through the stage door, across the wings and onto the stage at exactly the right moment for his first entrance. For months and months he reputedly did this!

Imagine the anxiety that this ego trip caused the stage manager, and the cast. Too many red lights, or a bottleneck on 48th Street, and the performance would have tanked. But this "star" felt that just showing up was all he had to do, with no concern about Preparing for his role, or the worries he was causing his colleagues.

Please: Recognize this behavior as selfish and inartistic, and conscientiously Prepare yourself for each entrance, at each performance.

But be careful. It's possible to go too far <u>the other way</u>: some very diligent people have been known to get so concentrated on Preparation that they didn't hear their entrance cues, and raced onto the stage late, with their careful Preparation in tatters, and their colleagues totally discombobulated. NoNoNo. Moderation in all things. To restate and clarify the admonition: **Prepare Well – AND - Listen for your Entrance Cue**.

*

## "Indicate" is a word of anathema in the theatre.

When I saw my son in a first-grade "health play," one of the kids was illustrating the need to have fresh air in the bedroom at night. He crossed to the imaginary window at Stage Left and pantomimed raising it – and he did a fine job of it, too.  He could have joined the cast of "Our Town," straightaway.  The trouble is that, at the same time he successfully pushed up the imaginary window, he said aloud:  "Open-Open."

This is indicating.  **Overstating your emotion, or state of mind**.

Wiping your brow with a big sweeping move, saying loudly, "Whew!" to indicate that you've just successfully escaped danger (or that it's terribly hot.)  Nix the big wipe and the big voice.

If you have a toothache or a broken ankle, you're always in pain, but life goes on, so you aren't constantly moaning, and petting the sore body part.  This, too, is indicating.  Better by far to favor the hurt place simply and naturally, without moans and groans.

The audience sees and hears everything, and will appreciate your not ridiculously maximizing the pain – or the heat – or the window opening.

On this topic (well, it really ISN'T, but it's an anecdote I like) – I saw a performance in which an actor answered the phone, but ignored the actual instrument directly in front of her and pantomimed grasping a phone, holding her hand to her ear, with her thumb and little finger sticking out.  Obviously, that theatre hadn't provided props until the last minute, and the actress had been pantomiming the phone in rehearsal for so long that she still did it even when there was an audience and a real phone.  That's Indicating that's even Worse than Indicating!

As you're building the emotional life of your character, **seek Depth, not Breadth**.  Dig into your character's viscera, rather than playing the externals.  This will help you to **create Drama, not Melodrama**.

Let your Anger sizzle in your belly, instead of manifesting itself in hyperbole by waving clenched fists and gasping for air.

Let your Love glow simply and brightly when your sweetheart enters, without a big sigh and silly smirk.

Let your Hatred smolder as you face your enemy, instead of hunching up your shoulders and clenching your jaw.

Leave the Indicating to six-year-olds. They're cute when they do it.

*

**You never want to be accused of "ham acting**," overplaying, "chewing the scenery" - <u>leaving truth or realism behind</u> while you enlarge your voice and movements into hyperbole. Never! Miss Galflong, that imaginary old-fashioned elocution teacher who will pop up here occasionally, might approve, but your director and your audiences in today's world will not. Keep it real, keep it truthful, keep it within your control.

*

**Stage Fright is your friend**. It keeps you centered, it makes you pay attention, it prevents you from becoming complacent.

Welcome it when it arrives, but not to the point that it incapacitates you.

Being prepared is the best defense against that fear of failure that stalks everyone in any line of work who really cares about doing a good job. Egotists who see the theatre merely as an opportunity to show off are rarely attacked by stage fright.

Be glad for that bottomless pit of anxiety right at the center of your stomach, and the hair on the back of your neck bristling with "Stage Awareness" (a more positive term than "fright"). This'll keep you focused on the moment, alert to the responsibilities at hand, and prevent you from ever "phoning it in;" that's why you're glad it's with you.

Laurence Olivier had terrible stage fright, and so did Alec Guinness, and they both had long, successful careers on stage, and were Knighted for their work. Olivier was even made a Lord, and Guinness was quoted as saying that stage fright was his best pal, for it kept him honest. You probably won't be honored by royalty, but you're in very good company in the metamorphosing of those negative feelings into positive performances, treating the audience as your close friends and co-creators.

### When you're least sure, be most positive.

This life-saving technique has probably been of great help to you at various points in your life – e.g., on a first date or at a job interview – and it will come to your aid with Stage Fright, or when anything goes wrong on stage.

If lines are missing (including your own), or a prop, or another actor, focus Not on the Fright that is generated, but instead on what you know that you know about the plot at this point along the Lightning Bolt.

Take a deep, relaxing breath, and what the heck, take another. Then, with your mind recovering even a few of the words or the actions that you remember occurring here, you can fill the gap and keep the play going. You may have to rewrite half a page, or create a prop out of a folded newspaper and a table lamp, or push three actors out the door, as you grab hold of that that solid recognizable Something that will put the play, and You, back on track.

You haven't given way to unsureness, or the "flop sweat" beginning to pour out of each pore, but you've moved positively to keep the action going, and the audience never knew that anything was wrong.

A faultless knowledge of your part, having thrown yourself into every minute of every rehearsal with all of your mind and body devoted to Thalia or Melpomene, the Muses of Comedy and Tragedy – and, oh, yes, those relaxing breaths - are the simplest, surest anti-fright medicines. (For some specifics, see Chapter 16)

*

Yeah-Yeah.  Least Sure – Most Positive.  Yeah-Yeah.  But **how about some solid help for when I lose my lines, when I "go up," or "dry,"** and none of my cast-mates is jumping in to save the day??

Miss Galflong said: "Picture the audience naked, so they seem vulnerable, and not likely to chase you across the state line." **This is terrible advice when you've "gone up,"** for it adds another layer of things for you to remember.  (And if you notice someone attractive in the House as you're imagining everyone nude, that's Another distraction.)

No, the best thing to know about the audience is that they don't have the playbook open in their laps, nor do they know what innovations the director might have introduced, so <u>They Have No Idea What You're Supposed to be Saying at This Moment</u>.  You have the gift of 30 seconds before someone out front recognizes that you've lost control.

So: let those reassuring deep breaths de-fog your mind. Then, as you calmly, in character, look out the window of the set, or into the fireplace, just roll the teleprompter behind your eyeballs to see if you can figure out where you lost the pattern.  The audience is still with you.  They can't tell that this isn't just a rehearsed pause, if you move with authority and a sense of knowing what you're doing. Perhaps you'll slowly pour yourself a drink, or loosen your tie, or fluff up your hair, with a thoughtful, introspective air which convinces them what a deep and sensitive character they're watching, when you're merely trying to remember the bloody line.

Even if you can't pick up the dialogue at the exact spot you lost it, you'll pinpoint the scene you're in, from the costume you're wearing, and who else is (or isn't) on stage with you. Good. **Latch onto the Next Recognizable Line** you can find in the jumble of your memory, put a capital letter at the beginning of it, and pronounce it with confidence, as if nothing had ever gone wrong.  And this line will propel you and your partners to the next, and you're back on track.

*

At a regional theatre conference, one of the conveners spoke about a similar conclave he'd attended a few weeks earlier in another part of the country: "What's the American theatre coming to?  I saw eight productions and only <u>two of them</u> were <u>perfect</u>."

I replied that he was luckier than I.  I'd directed a hundred and fifty, and None of them was perfect.  He was dumbstruck.  "But - why do you stay in the theatre, then?"

"Because I keep trying."

And so we must.  But while trying with all our might, I really believe, and I hope to help you believe, too, that we won't settle for easy "perfection," accepting a half-done creation, when in our hearts we know we've got a long way to go, and are willing to dedicate ourselves to that journey.

One of my teachers emphasized that **"<u>too many actors mistake getting Better for getting Good</u>."**

And Anton Chekhov, as he was very good at doing, gave us the clearest instructions:  **"<u>Dissatisfaction with oneself is one of the foundation stones of every real talent</u>."**

\*

A sarcastic director may sometime advise you to stop at the Prop Table to pick up some **<u>Stage Presence</u>.**

Well, of course you won't find it there, or anyplace other than in your own body and mind and heart.

It means bringing to the stage a total, well-composed assurance that lets the audience know that you Belong there, and that they're in good hands.

It begins with knowing what you're doing:  Learning your lines (and, when applicable, your songs and dances) letter-perfectly, letting them grow from the character's emotion, and combining them with the blocking you've rehearsed with the director.

Stage Presence includes:

carrying your instruments (your Voice and your Body) proudly, in perfect condition, well-tuned and sufficiently warmed up within the last few minutes;

your confidence that with perfect ease you'll be able to hit those high notes or bark out that rasping accusatory shout, and still have a smooth and well-controlled voice for the rest of the performance;

your easy belief that you are fully in charge: of your hands and your arms, in repose as well as when you're using them to illustrate a point or an emotion . . . . and of your feet and your legs, standing comfortably without shifting your weight, and then readily crouching or running, as your blocking demands.

You are Present, and you are Ready.

*

### "I'm not going to Tell you; I'm going to Show you."

This was the motivating line of a story told by a theatre philosopher who imagined that the first theatre performance wasn't given by the Greeks or even the Egyptians as some scholars believe – but by a cave man in prehistory who, when asked by the chieftain to tell the tribe about the hunt he'd just been on, said: "No. That would be boring." *(Let's accept the fact that these guys knew pretty well how to communicate with each other, so we'll avoid the usually-accepted denigrating "Ugh"s and "Oooga"s.)* "And the hunt wasn't boring; it was exciting. So I won't Tell you, but I'll Show you."

And he directed one of his buddies to put on the skin of the sabre-toothed tiger whose meat they had just eaten, to help him act out the hunt, giving the children and the elderly a true feeling of what it felt like to track and kill their dinner.

That's what we do, too. It's not an easy chair or podium (or cave) that we occupy, from which we Tell the audience our story, but a Stage, upon which we Show them our characters' feelings, conflicts and the resolving of those conflicts. If at any moment on stage you realize that your audience could attain the same level of entertainment by just reading the script at home, you'd better check to see if your tiger skin is properly situated.

*

## The show must go on.

That's a cliché you've probably heard many times and, like most clichés, it has a basis in fact.

Each member of an audience has made a conscious decision to come to your performance. Maybe someone just decided today, while someone else has been looking forward to it for a long time. Several patrons paid a lot of money, and some bought inexpensive tickets, and a few even got in free.

Here's a friend of someone in the cast, and that lady was attracted by the fine reputation of this theatre, and the man in the t-shirt just came on a whim.

No matter what or how or why, they all deserve to see the show that has been advertised, and for which he took a shower and she put on jewelry, and they made a definite point of being there, in their seats, reading their programs, at the announced curtain time.

If someone in the cast or crew is ill, or (Heaven forfend) has died, or if there's been a calamity in the theatre building, from fire or burst pipes, or if a snowstorm has blanketed the city, making it difficult for you to reach the theatre - - The show must still Go On.

Maybe someone has to commandeer a city snowplow and ride it into the suburbs to pick up a stranded actor, or the director has to play a role with script in hand, or a damaged section of the House has to be roped off because the seats are unseatable; or the electricity has died and the ushers have been instructed to direct their flashlights onto the stage, focused on whoever is speaking; or massive portable heaters are brought in because the boiler has blown up. Fine. I've done each of those things to keep a show alive, and every experienced theatre person can tell even more grisly stories of how, no matter what, the show went on.

As an actor, you wouldn't be responsible for making such decisions, but your opinion may be asked if there's a possibility of canceling a performance, and I hope you'll say: "Never!"

There've been several wobbly equations invented to justify suspending a performance: if less than ten percent of the seating capacity has arrived, or if the size of the audience outnumbers the cast; or there's no difference between indoor and outdoor temperatures, or there's a major impending storm.   It's as if reasons are actively sought to abandon the play.

I say: "Pfui!"  And I say: "Yes, The Show Must Always Go On."  Our audience expects it and deserves it.

\*

# Chapter 3

# STAGE DIRECTIONS

As with any profession, we have many arcane words and phrases in the Theatre particular (and peculiar) to our craft, so that we can communicate with each other clearly and succinctly. These begin with **STAGE DIRECTIONS**.

A <u>Proscenium Stage</u> **is a traditional platform at one end of an auditorium** (The "House"), often with a curtain that opens and closes behind the Proscenium Arch, the picture frame separating the stage from the audience, whose seats all face the performance space foursquare.

On a Proscenium Stage, remember that **Left and Right are always determined by the** <u>actor's</u> **Left and Right**, facing the audience – NOT the audience's Left and Right.

Remember, too, that **Upstage and Downstage** are terms handed down from many years ago when things were reversed: the audience's seats were all on one flat floor, so for better visibility the <u>stage</u> was tilted, or raked, with the back end higher than the front. <u>That back end was called "Upstage" (because it was up high), and the end closer to the audience, and down low, was "Downstage</u>." And so it is today.

Side-to-side locations were added to these terms. For instance, "**Down Left**," means to the actor's <u>own</u> Left and near the audience. "**Up Right**" then of course would be farther back from the audience, and to the actor's own Right.

Center, thankfully, is "**Center**," so "**Down Center**" means the front of the stage, and midway from side to side.

Exponential multiplication will then give us, for instance: **"Up Left Center," "Down Right," "Up Center,"** etcetc.

And, making it even easier for actors to record the blocking in their scripts, these terms are most often abbreviated: **DL, UR, C, DC, ULC, DR, UC, etcetc**, to the ends of the earth, or at least to the edges of the stage. (Here is their placement, in <u>Figure 4</u>.)

\*

---

| UR | UC | UL |
|----|----|----|
| URC | C | ULC |
| DR | DC | DL |

<u>audience</u>

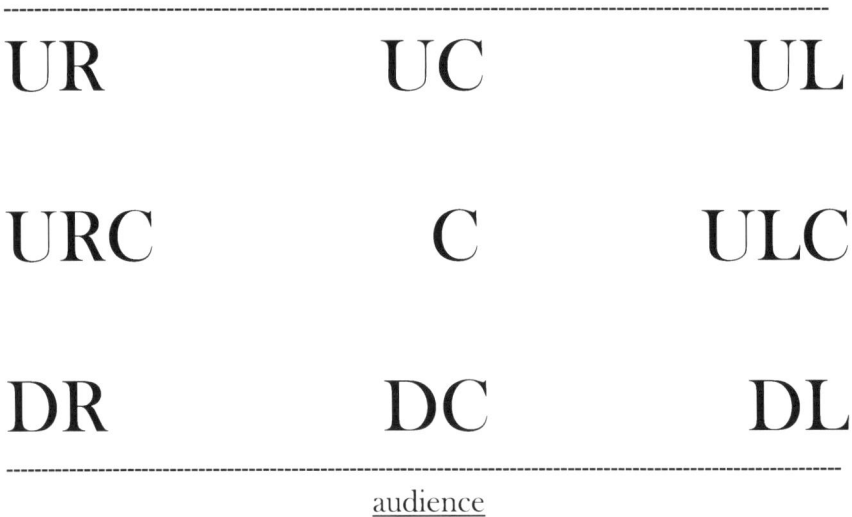

Figure 4. **Stage Directions.**

In an **Arena Theatre, or Theatre-in-the-Round** (around which the audience sits, in the entire 360 degrees) or a **Thrust Stage** (similar to Shakespeare's Globe Theatre, with the audience located ¾ of the way around the stage, giving the actors, the director and the set designer one single back wall of scenery to work with, for doors and windows and to establish color, period, dimensionality, etc) the Stage Directions are sometimes given the same as on a Proscenium Stage – UL, DRC, etc – but often, instead, the director chooses to see the stage as the **Face of a Clock,** with **"12 o'clock"** in the Up Center position on a Thrust, and in an arbitrary "Up Center" in an Arena, probably determined by the juxtaposition of the Lobby, or the Dressing Rooms, or some other landmark of that building.

From 12 o'clock, then, naturally the Stage Directions proceed clockwise around the perimeter of the stage, from 1 o'clock down to 6 o'clock (in the Down Center location) and ending up back at 12.

The actor's blocking would be written into the script as "Sit in 3 o'c chair" or "X to 2 o'c end of sofa," etc.

\*

A **Black Box Theatre** is a small room that usually seats less than 100 patrons and can be configured into Any of the above layouts, or even widely diverse relationships between actors and audience, by moving platforms and seats to satisfy the needs of the production.

\*

# Chapter 4

# AUDITIONS

Before you walk into the audition room or onto its stage, hoping that your talent (and your physical type) will win you a role in a play, take a seat for a moment on a nearby bench, which I've conveniently imagined there for you.

*(If you're a professional actor, and a role will be accompanied by a paycheck, then forget this imaginary bench, and go on into the auditions. And Break a Leg! For everyone else:)*

Sit down.

Take a deep breath.

Remind yourself of all the commitments already demanding your time and energy and focus. Family. Classes. Job. Volunteer work, etc. Important claimants of your close attention and large hunks of your days and evenings.

And then say to yourself:
"**Rehearsing and Performing a Play takes a Long, Long, Long Time.**"
From first rehearsal to closing night, you'll be heavily involved for weeks, if not months. Even a small role will demand your presence a lot!

The rewards of theatre are overwhelming, in creativity, friendship, fun, and getting out of yourself into another human being's skin. You'll never forget the breakthrough moments in rehearsal, or the audience's big laugh, or sustained applause, or stunned silence at a crucial point in the play. Acting provides a joy unlike almost anything else on earth.

But: Can you afford to Give all that the theatre Demands in exchange? How's your health, for example?

Reviewing seriously all these aspects of your life vs a major time commitment during the coming weeks, **if you are sure that you Can't Not do it**, then charge into that Audition, and wow them, and prepare for **one of the greatest experiences of your life**!

*

**AND:::** Approach **every Audition firstly as an Adventure in itself.** If you enjoy the theatre, the experience of the audition alone can be a delight. You'll be with other theatre people, reading aloud from a script by an excellent (we hope) playwright, or participating in an improvisation to show your imaginative skills, or performing a monologue or a song which you've previously rehearsed. In whichever form it takes, have a ball!

**But when it's over, go home and forget about it**! This adventure was great fun, but now It's Over!

If you replay the audition in your mind, visiting again your good moments and what you may wrongly consider your less-good moments, you'll drive yourself crazy. And if you sit staring at the telephone, waiting for a call from the theatre, you <u>are</u> crazy.

**The adventure is Over.**

There are dozens of reasons why Actor A is cast over Actor B, and many times it <u>has nothing to do with Talent</u>. A friend of mine got his first Broadway role because he was shorter than the star, who was 5'6" tall and quite paranoid about his height. Another had been told that a role was his [but with no contract signed yet] in a road company of "Mame," replacing an actor who was ill, but he quickly lost the job five minutes later when a phone call advised that the costumes already on the way to Chicago were several sizes smaller than he.

So forget about how well you did. That may have very little to do with it. That adventure has come and gone. Focus on other, palpable, aspects of your life.

But – Now – Hey – Wait! If you get a call to come back for a further audition, or telling you that <u>You've Been Cast in the Play</u>, then Hooray! <u>Another</u> Adventure will begin.

<u>But never count on it, and Please: Never let your heart break if you're Not cast.</u>

*

# <u>OK.  So how do you prepare for an Audition</u>?

<u>Learn all you can about the role ahead of time</u>, from information the theatre has provided, and from thorough research, and of course from <u>the actual script of the play</u>, if you can get one.

Choose a character (or several) that you <u>realistically</u> could play.  What Age is the director looking for in this role, what Body Type, what Special Skills (e.g. tap dancing, rope-twirling, trumpet playing, etc.)?
Does the role require a command of poetry, or a specific Dialect (Southern, German, etc)?

If you prepare yourself properly, and assess <u>honestly</u> your appropriateness for the role you want, you can arrive with confidence, showing the director your initiative, and you won't embarrass yourself by asking to read for a part you obviously wouldn't fit.

<u>Wear clothing similar to what you think the character would wear</u>, or at least giving the line and feeling of the role, and the same period, if different from today.  No, please, <u>not an actual Costume</u>, but something simple that helps the director imagine you in that situation.  A long skirt, a tailored blouse, a rakish hat, a patterned necktie, heavy boots, bright colors, or the like.

<u>If you're allowed to select your own audition material</u>, probably a monologue, choose carefully.  Never give a passage from the play being cast; that's just too risky, because the director probably has her own idea how she wants that speech given.

Find a passage from <u>another play</u> that provides:

- Variety, with at least one solid Transition.
- The same style as the play you're auditioning for.
- The same period as this play.
- A chance to show off <u>your best qualities</u>: e.g., freewheeling humor, stark drama, range of speaking voice, clarity of Transitions, etc.

And, indeed, it's a very good idea to have memorized, and kept in the forefront of your mind, <u>several</u> monologues, because you never know when, at an audition, a director will say to you: "Yes, that's good.  What else can you show me?"

Sadly, if you have Nothing to show, you're admitting your unsuitability to take your place in a production rife with forward-thinking and *well-prepared* theatre people.

If you intend to audition frequently, and for myriad types of plays, it's a good idea – No, it's a Necessity - to arm yourself with well-rehearsed and solidly-memorized monologues of these styles:

- **Modern drama** [Plays by Edward Albee, Adam Rapp, Tom Stoppard, etc]
- **Modern comedy** [Neil Simon, Alan Ayckbourn, Tom Stoppard (again!)]
- **Classical drama** [Shakespeare, Sophocles, Chekhov]
- **Classical comedy** [Shakespeare (again), Beaumont & Fletcher, Goldoni]

\*

Many professional Casting Directors have said frankly that "It's not <u>us</u> who cast the roles.  **Actors themselves do the casting, by bringing to us qualities that we realize will best suit the characters.**"

Indeed, most characters could be interpreted in any one of <u>several</u> ways, and if you show yourself off at your best, with a solid point of view and an evident understanding of the role, you're likely to convince the director that This is the way the part should be played, and that You are the one to play it.

*

### If you can only see yourself as a dashing Leading man or a pert and sophisticated Leading woman, you're going to miss out on playing some of the best roles ever written.

Many Supporting roles are marvelous to play, while some Romantic leads, especially, are painfully Dull!  Romeo and Juliet are always sighing and complaining, a couple of lovesick twerps.

But Mercutio!  Or the Nurse! Ah, either one is a part to sink your teeth into.  No, they haven't as much stage-time as R&J, but they have Dimension, and Laugh-lines, and Great Character Traits . . . and they enter, play their scenes, and then get the heck offstage - often accompanied by rich applause.  (And they have far fewer lines to learn!!)

It's said that Shakespeare had to kill Mercutio off so early in the play because he was beginning to steal the show from Romeo!! That's the kind of part you want to play!

Whereas, if you insist on auditioning only for a Lead, you might be out in the cold, while less egocentric actors are having the time of their lives, in smaller roles.

*

### Whenever the director or stage manager speaks at Auditions, Listen to every word, and do your best to comply with

any requirements or limitations of this tryout session, such as:  How much time you're allowed – and whether you should introduce yourself or the title of your audition piece – and whether you should stay after you've finished, etc.

Too often, overly-confident actors don't listen carefully or, in spite of what they've heard, they think: "Sure! Sure!  Well, wait till they get a look at what I can do; they won't worry about those silly rules."   Say Goodbye right now, if that's your attitude.

\*

**One of the most basic skills a director will expect of an actor is the ability to be Heard by every member of the audience,** and you must demonstrate your mastery of projecting your voice at this audition.

If the director can't hear you, you'll be written off, and won't have another chance at winning the role.

The more kind-hearted directors may understand that you're speaking into a new and unfamiliar House, and simply call out to you: "Volume!"   This of course does <u>not</u> mean that you should Yell, but rather open your throat, support your words, and Project them clearly straight at that person out in the darkness who has the ability to make you very happy by casting you.

\*

**Be agreeable to anything (legal) that the director asks.**

Could you learn to do a cartwheel in the next few weeks? Juggle?  Play the trombone?  Ride a unicycle?  Memorize a long passage in an unfamiliar language?

If you know from experience that you Can't do this thing being asked, if, for instance you're tone-deaf, or have two left feet, then of course it would be folly to volunteer for, or agree to, something that you know you'd fail.

Otherwise, your answer must be:  "Of Course I could!!"  Or as a confident middle-aged woman once proclaimed to me from an audition stage: "Not YET!"  Oh, Yes, she was cast.  And did well.

\*

If you and all the other hopeful actors are sitting in the same room with the director, perhaps auditioning more than once when called upon, **you can make yourself into a big nuisance by asking to read too many times.**  Uh-Uh!

It's the mark of an inexperienced actor to believe that: "If I can do it Just One More Time, I can nail this role."

Oh, my, No!  Please trust each director to have already knocked off 10% for your nervousness and 20% for feeling that they haven't explained the role sufficiently - - so you may in fact be rating very highly.  But if you keep waving your hand and squeaking, it'll seem to be evident that you'll bring this same irritating quality to rehearsals - and nobody will deliberately cast a disruptive actor.

*

On the other hand:  Because there are so many people auditioning – lots of them looking very much like you - **make yourself memorable**, without being a pain in the neck.

If you know that the director had a recent success with "My Fair Lady," you might say: "I get the feeling that this character is sort of a diamond in the rough, like Eliza Doolittle; would that be a good way to approach her?" or "Henry Higgins' egotism came to mind when I saw this fellow's description; would I be right in starting with that idea?"  Questions like these don't steal time from the reading, yet imprint you favorably on the director's mind.

If you wear glasses, show up on stage Without them, to let everyone see what you look like, and then, just before you read, reach into your big, colorful, tote bag and (quickly) pull out your charming but maybe very large spectacles, so you can read the script - - thus imprinting both the big bag and the big glasses on the producers' memories, in addition to your own winningly bare face.

Wear a simple, flattering, and eye-catching accessory – such as a bright-green scarf or necktie – and then wear it at each successive audition, making it a personal reminder that sets you apart from everyone else.

As you're making all these decisions at home, before heading for auditions, make an important choice **Not to embarrass yourself**.

No apologizing because "I have a cold, and can't hit the high notes today," or "I forgot my tap shoes," or "I thought I could read Spanish better than that." Think before you speak.

If you're going to be out of town for the week before the play opens, it would be wrong to even offer yourself at tryouts. They aren't going to conduct Dress Rehearsals without you.

If the script contains some words that you will not say, or a love scene that you will not participate in, please stay home, away from a no-win situation.

I remember an audition in which a young lady was presenting a monologue that none of us on the staff was familiar with, when suddenly she whipped off her dress, revealing herself in a blue-ribbon-adorned bustier. The stripping was, it turned out, called for in her script – but it bloody well wasn't necessary for her audition. This costume was perfectly decent, and didn't show a lot of skin, but it Was underwear, and was the sort of surprise that is less pleasant than she'd hoped, and she could tell from our dead silence that she'd made a mistake. When her reading finally, blessedly, ended, she had to collect all her belongings, including her dress, from the floor, and scamper offstage, half-clad.

And she didn't get the role.

Consider wisely about how to be memorable at an Audition.

*

If it becomes evident to you that someone else has caught the director's eye, and you realize that you're not really in contention for the role you've sought, **consider offering yourself as an Understudy**.

Though illness and accident (and laryngitis) lurk all around us, too many producers and directors wait too long before thinking about "covering" the major roles, or indeed ANY of the roles, with understudies who are rehearsed to the point of being ready to go onstage if needed.  Perhaps they'll realize their neglect when you authoritatively offer yourself as an understudy, perhaps for several roles.

If you're brought into the company in this position, you'll have the benefit of attending all the rehearsals, hearing all the direction, and, though you may rarely if ever get into the action, you'll be a solid part of the production.

If you're wise, you'll be able to demonstrate what a valuable member of the ensemble you are, helping another actor with his lines, and of course hopping right onto the stage or rehearsal floor when one of the actors you're understudying is having photos taken elsewhere or being interviewed by the newspaper.

And Cinderella stories do happen.  After the play has opened, you may have the opportunity to go on at one or more performances.  **Be sure you're ready!** Watch the scenes that involve your character(s) every time, and run the lines for yourself every day.

With all that, the odds still are that you'll never go on.  I was understudying seven roles in a Broadway show, and one of my guys, an older gentleman, broke his collarbone.  I felt sincerely bad for him, but - - - Oh, Joy! My big chance!!
 But, No – He merely had his costumes moved into the stage-level boiler room, so he didn't have to climb the stairs to his regular dressing room - and he never missed a performance. THAT's the most likely scenario.

But so what?  Nothing is ever wasted, and even if you never appear on stage you've had the opportunity to prepare one or more roles, with all the creativity and ensemble work that that offers, and you made yourself useful and friendly to the company, so you'll be remembered as a valuable asset, when a future production is casting. That's a very positive result of your work.

*

# Chapter 5

# <u>REHEARSALS</u>

Very few new buildings, whether private homes or office blocks, are completed and ready to move into on the date promised by the contractors.

Some authors, even when their contracts exact penalties for late delivery, hand over their manuscripts to the publisher many months late.

But we in the theatre have no such leeway. **<u>If we sell tickets for a production to open at 8 p.m. on May 1, there are going to be people sitting in the House at that time on that date</u>** who are not going to accept a sheepish director peeping out from a corner of the proscenium arch, saying, "We're not quite ready.  Go home."

Some theatres, generally summer or winter stock, rehearse a complete play in just one week.  Others spend two weeks in rehearsals, others four, or even five or more.  And as the great theatre genius Stanislavski was reported to have said after a Year in rehearsal: "**<u>Just two more days, please</u>**." No production arguably <u>ever</u> has enough rehearsal time, but we know at the beginning exactly how long we have to prepare, and the director carefully apportions our work over the days or weeks, so the first curtain opens at the time specified, with (usually) a well-rehearsed, ready-to-be-seen performance.  But if we only had just two more days!!

*

For years, when casts that I was directing hit low spots, when each rehearsal was just a repetition of the previous one with no growth, no inspiration, no sharpening and tightening, I would give a pep talk, urging the actors to keep in mind the **<u>derivation of the word</u>** "<u>rehearsal</u>."  It means a "re-hearing," I told them, in which we hear the playwright's words <u>afresh</u> each day, which stirs us to make each re-hearing solider, deeper, more stageworthy than the last.

Then one night, driving home after rehearsal, I realized that this exhortation wasn't working, even for me; that it was thin and uninspiring. So later that night I went to my dictionary to see if there was some stronger ammunition available. Well, Yeah! There was! **I was wrong!** I should have researched it long before.

### "Rehearse" Doesn't mean "re-hear."  It means "re-harrow".

That's what the Old French language has passed on to us.

"Harrowing" is what farmers do to the hard ground, to make it suitable for seeding.  The harrow is a frame that holds sharp teeth, pulled across a field, ruthlessly slicing up the land, again and again, with an aim toward ultimate growth and fruitfulness.

So each rehearsal actually is a <u>Re-Harrowing</u>, another wonderful opportunity to dig and slice and claw through the elements of the play, seeking new approaches, solidifying the better scenes and replacing those that aren't working or have become stale amid more affecting and affective moments.

So please realize as I did, but <u>sooner</u> than I did: If you approach each rehearsal with a vivid image of slashing through dead ground, churning it up, and bringing new life to your role, it'll have the proper chance to grow into the beautiful work of art you had in mind when you started.

Otherwise, you'll find yourself focusing on the "hearse" syllable of "rehearse."

*

## OK.  Now how do you Prepare for your First Rehearsal?

After you're cast and as soon as you're given your script, underline or highlight all your lines, and stay close to your dictionary and encyclopaedia, those between covers or those on line, to **check the exact meaning and pronunciation of every word and phrase** that's unfamiliar to you, not just those in your lines, but in the entire show. There's no shame in seeking help from reference sources, and every reason why you should, as part of your contribution to the excellence of the play, and to your own role.

I'm laughing (and cringing) as I write this, remembering stark mispronunciations I've heard in performances, which should have been caught at first rehearsal – No, even before first rehearsal. Here are a few. Imagine the worst possible mangling of these words, and you'll hear what I heard:
"*archipelago*," "*poetaster*," "*desuetude*," and both "*Pontius*" and "*Pilate*."

You're right, of course - These aren't everyday words. Hey, playwrights are literate folks, and rightly enjoy using unusual and evocative vocabulary when the situation calls for it, and it's up to every actor to bring those words to life – accurately. Even if you think you might know the meaning of a particularly arcane word, Doubt Yourself, and look it up - but do it early, before you've irrevocably implanted the wrong pronunciation in your brain. (And I've heard that word, too, mangled on stage, as "ih-re-VOKE-uh-blee.")

Your playwright and your director have both done a great deal of research, to learn everything they can to make the story, the plot, come alive.
You should do no less. **You should research, too**: the period, the country, the manners and morals, the occupation of your character, and read other works by this same playwright . . . so you're doing your part [pun not intended, but gratefully accepted] to flesh out every moment you're on stage, knowing all you can about the environment, the atmosphere, the people of the play.

*

And now's the time to begin finding your Transitions – The graceful evolving from one emotion to another, caused by a stimulus, internal (The character realizes that she's alone in the spooky, dead quiet, dark room) or external (She hears a blood-curdling scream).

**<u>The audience travels on your Transitions, step by step through the play, and on up the Lightning Bolt.</u>**   This is a very important point for you to remember, and to work with, always. You've got to let the audience clearly know when you're transitioning - changing - from Love to Hate, e.g., or Anger to Fear, or they'll be lost and confused, and would do better to take home a copy of the script and read the play quietly to themselves.

I used to enjoy watching television dramas with my mother, who would speak out loud her thoughts about the acting: "Oh, he didn't like that," "Awww, she's getting interested in him," "Ooo, they're really scared now," etc. She was sweet and funny, but she was also <u>correct</u>! Her audible remarks are <u>exactly the thoughts and feelings</u> that we want to generate, consciously or subconsciously, within the heads and hearts of every member of the audience, Transition by Transition. We hope they won't shout them out, as my mother did, but maybe that would actually be a good thing, once in a while. It'd really let us know how we're doing, in moving the play and the character along up the Lightning Bolt, emotion-to-Transition-to-emotion-to-Transition, and so on gloriously through the performance.

*

Here's a break-down:

### <u>The Three Parts of a Transition are</u>:

- **<u>Receive</u>** <u>the stimulus, the information</u> (e.g. The kiss, the gunshot, the news that Juliet is dead, the internal realization that you don't love your boyfriend any more.)

<u>THEN</u>:

- **<u>Digest</u>** <u>the information</u> (take a quiet moment – or several – to swallow it, and slowly recognize that it's true, as you let go of the <u>old</u> emotion)

**THEN:**

- **React** to the information. This is the completion of the Transition, as you slide into the new emotion (Loving the kiss and the kisser, or becoming deathly afraid of the man with the gun, or deeply sorrowful at the loss of your sweet new girlfriend) and let that carry you forward into the next steps of the plot.

The evolution between emotions, this three-part Transition, is like a steep Chinese arched bridge. You receive the stimulus, as you gently ascend the rounded arch of the bridge within your existing emotion, and digest the stimulus, quietly at rest at the Top of the bridge, and then react to it as you descend the far side of the bridge into the new emotion, arriving at the bottom completely within the new emotion.

This technique can also be illustrated in this way: Slowly Inhale from the old emotion, then make the Transition as your breath is being momentarily held, and then Exhale out into the new emotion.

But the audience MUST be conscious of each Transition, and each Step of each Transition - or they won't know where they are. It's a subtler, more structured version of the clichéd "light-bulb going on, above your head."

As you find the potential stimuli and their ensuing Transitions before rehearsals begin, mark them in your script - in Pencil, because undoubtedly some will change through rehearsals, as the play and your character grow. But it's important for you to have spotted them early, and underscored them, so you can start rehearsal with at least a basic idea of where your character is going.

It's easier to Transition from Something, than from Nothing. And it'll be smoother for you to find New and More Useful Transitions in rehearsal, if you've already spotted where you feel that a Transition should begin.

*

Something else to mark in your script, also in pencil, **are your character's Thought Groups**, sequential lines of dialogue usually on the same subject, though the fact that these are called "Thought" groups indicates that you're seeking what goes Behind the overt lines of dialogue, and not necessarily said out loud.

As you read through your role many times at home, you'll get the feeling of your character's focus in each scene, and note the single topic that is at the center of the character's concentration in each sequence of lines, and recognize that the dialogue, even when it's not specifically on that subject, grows from and enhances its Thought Group.

Some examples might be: "I'm disgusted with this guy;" "She's really a terrific woman;" "Why hasn't Pat come home yet?" "I'm having more fun at this party than I'd expected;" "If I have to spend one more second in this house, I'll scream!"

Clearly mark the beginning and ending of each Thought Group, which usually will last a minute or so, though some Thought Groups will occupy only a single line, and some may continue for several pages. Unless the script is non-representational, your dialogue will proceed naturally, building on your and other peoples' lines, entrances and exits, underscored by Thought Groups.

Very likely, the end of a Thought Group will coincide with the stimulus that will trigger a Transition into a new emotion, as well as into a new Thought Group.

This approach to your script helps you to build your character's Lightning Bolt, moving upward through the performance, and makes it much easier to learn your lines, since each line stems from its particular Thought Group. This is also a strong bulwark against forgetting your lines ("Going Up") on stage because, knowing which Thought Group generated the contiguous lines will keep you centered, and, should you have a momentary lapse, will assist you to resume your smooth recall of your dialogue – or the basic Theme of your dialogue - more quickly and securely.

In classical or poetic plays, you'll surely find long speeches, and even in contemporary realistic works there're often some hefty monologues, that seem to fill the page and make you wonder how you'll get through them.

No problem. As you work with your script at home, break them down to **identify each successive Thought Group,** and mark them off – with a pencil, as always, for rehearsals may cause these decisions, too, to grow and change.

As well as making the speech easier to memorize, it'll more importantly help you communicate to the audience its import, and what it's based on in your character's inner life, <u>thought by thought</u>.

And remember: going into and out of each Thought Group, you'll almost certainly want to impose a Transition.

*

**<u>You should spend as many hours working on your role, alone, away from rehearsal, as you do At rehearsal.</u>** I think that explains itself. And it's a vital self-assignment.

*

Equally as important as what you think, and what you say, is **<u>How do you say it?</u>**
Some of the finest plays, both classical and contemporary, are in fact long Poems; and some of the finest language in Prose plays is absolutely first-rate poetry.

<u>How does your director want you to handle the poetry?</u> Focusing carefully on the meter and the rhymes? Or treating it more as everyday speech, knowing that the poetic rhythm will always be there, adding its beauty to the dialogue (illustrating one definition of poetry as "prose read in front of a waterfall")? Follow exactly the director's wishes.

On your own, you'll want to single out every image in your dialogue, whether in the roughshod speech of Stanley Kowalski or a timeless soliloquy of Electra, and ascertain what the playwright intended to convey, and <u>how you can best bring this poetic imagery to your audience</u>, in keeping with the style of the production the director is creating, and the consistency of your character as you build it.

*

**<u>Where did you come from</u>**?  No, this isn't a timorous conversation about conception, but a necessary question for you to answer preceding each entrance you make in the play.

<u>Where has your character **just been** before appearing on stage</u>?  And "in my dressing room" is the wrong answer.

It will make a huge difference in the emotion you bring on stage if you've just been driving home from work anticipating a big hug and kiss from your husband, or if you were watering the lawn and saw a horrific auto wreck right in front of your house.

Romeo had just eavesdropped on his carousing friends making bawdy jokes as he disgustedly climbed over the wall into the moonlit garden under Juliet's balcony. <u>There's</u> a Transition for you!!

Hamlet, at the top of Act V, arriving at the grave being prepared for the body of Ophelia, carries with him all that has happened to him offstage: He was tricked into going to England with Rosencrantz and Guildenstern, where he would be executed, but their ship was attacked by pirates, who made away with Hamlet. They turned out to be friendly pirates who brought him safely back to Denmark.  These adventures (brought to life by stimuli from your own experiences) are the specific off-stage events that you must bring onstage, as you learn of Ophelia's death.

*

**<u>After the Costume Designer has described, or shown you a sketch of, what your costume(s) will be like, you should wear similar clothing at every rehearsal</u>**, to accustom yourself from the very first as to how your clothing will feel on your body, in performance.

Actors who wear tennis shoes and blue jeans to rehearse a character who in the performances will be wearing leather dress shoes and military trousers, or hoop skirts and high lace-up shoes, will have an enormously difficult time adjusting, when dress rehearsal begins.

Sir Laurence Olivier said that he approached every role by finding the proper Nose for his character. We simpler folk may not want a different nose for every play, but in fact should start wearing the proper Shoes from first rehearsal onwards, building the physicality of the character From the Ground Up.

You know very well how differently you walk and stand and carry yourself in stiff leather shoes, or riding boots, hiking boots, and high heels, or low heels, and, Yes, tennis shoes.

Equally important are the use of rehearsal skirts of the actual length of your costumes, and similar jackets, hats, and gloves. It makes no difference what they Look like in the rehearsal room, just what they Feel like, helping you move from yourself into the full physical presence of your character.

If it's a period play, the women may be wearing actual corsets, to give the proper look to their costumes and carriage to their bodies. If so, then believe me, you'll want to start wearing a corset at the earliest possible rehearsal, for they take a long time to get used to, in walking and sitting, and even standing still. Not to mention breathing, and possibly inhibiting projecting your lines into the heart of the House.

And, for goodness' sake, if you'll be wearing any sort of padding, to make you look heavier, or to appear pregnant, get hold of the actual padding, or the best possible substitute, and wear it at every rehearsal.

If you are directed to wear or carry **props or costume pieces** that you're unaccustomed to, such as eyeglasses, swords, rings, bracelets, and the like, **start using suitable stand-ins early**, or you'll find yourself absently fiddling with the unfamiliar real item during performances.

I'm sure you've seen, on stage or screen, an actor who keeps adjusting her glasses, or on-and-off clutches at the handle of the sword at his side, betraying the newness of these items that should be totally familiar to the character.  Distracting!  Disappointing!

People who deal with such items every day do it without consciously realizing these things are hanging on their bodies – and that's precisely the ease you must seek and attain.

Early in the rehearsal period, the Stage Manager will probably bring rehearsal substitutes for every prop in the show (often just magazines, soda bottles, small boxes, or pieces of wood – something approximating the size, shape and weight of all the real props) so you and the director can grow accustomed to your handling something tangible at the proper moments.

**This is especially necessary with liquids.  Start using them early.** The timing of your lines will naturally be affected by handling and pouring "liquor," "coffee," etc, and by drinking them.  If you add liquid late in the rehearsal period, your timing will have to be totally readjusted, wasting everyone's time.  Water is the only liquid you need for rehearsals, representing every liquid.

If the SM doesn't have everything on hand for you, then **it's up to you to provide yourself with something** to wear or handle or pour, as soon as possible.

\*

Many playwrights will describe every character down to height and weight, and each facial mole, the exact hair color, and three generations of ancestors.  But please believe that **you are Not honor-bound to obey all the stage directions,** emotional demands, and character descriptions that are printed in your script.  That was Then, this is Now.  That was a different theatre, a different audience, a different set of scenery, a different time (perhaps even a different Century!).

If you're lucky enough to have the playwright at your rehearsals, you (or better, your director) can ask why certain movements or mannerisms, or vital statistics, were called for. Otherwise, which of course is usually the case, use any of the author's notations that are <u>helpful</u> to you in realizing your character amid the Concept and Interpretation of this director, in this city, and this time in history.

**The rest – abandon them.**

*

### <u>If you're not 10 minutes early, you're 10 minutes late</u>.

Whenever the Call Time is for you to check in at rehearsal, anticipate it by at least 10 minutes.

This is the standard rule of timing around the world, for the very good reason that very few plays in history have had <u>too much</u> rehearsal.

Every minute is precious, and if you're just 5 minutes late, keeping a cast of 10 waiting, that's *5 minutes x 10 people = <u>50</u> minutes wasted,* lost forever. And you've driven the Stage Manager crazy, trying to locate you, so rehearsal can begin.

The Call Time, when you're due to begin rehearsal, doesn't mean getting out of your car at that minute, or combing your hair in the rest room, or calling your agent or your baby-sitter – but <u>in the rehearsal area</u>, <u>warmed up</u>, <u>in rehearsal clothing for this scene</u>, and with <u>script or prop in hand</u>, <u>ready to work</u> - 10 minutes early.

Or, absolutely, you're now 10 minutes Late, and that's inexcusable.

*

**<u>Learn your lines</u>.** To many civilians (non-theatre people) this is all there is to acting, and they think it's a mysterious gift. "How do you memorize All Those Words?" Well, you know that <u>it's the tiniest part of the craft of acting</u> - BUT until those lines are solidly in your memory-bank you can't really tap the needed emotions, nor fully start to carve out the character - so learn them early.  And accurately.  Delay in line-learning inhibits your full participation in the rehearsals, and slapdash or late memorization is arrant thoughtlessness toward the rest of the cast. It's the first thing required of every actor, and "required" is too mild a word.

Memorization is a chore, but a lovely chore, for it's freeing you to create the character and the emotions, day by day.  And big speeches, particularly, must be learned right away, because they don't involve a give-and-take with another character, but are solely your responsibility to bring to rehearsal, tucked verbatim in a corner of your mind.

**Learn your Cues** simultaneously with learning your lines. These are the few words (or an action) that precede each line of yours, and catapult you into speaking. If you know all of your dialogue letter-perfectly, but don't know when you're supposed to say it - - - Disaster!

After working alone with the script, and committing a Scene or an Act to memory pretty accurately, most actors then solidify their memorization by having someone "hear their lines."  A family member or long-suffering friend can usually be recruited for this job, and other cast members, or the Assistant Stage Manager, may also be willing to sit with you somewhere quiet and read you each successive Cue, and make sure that the lines you reply are exactly what is in the script.  This helps tie the Cue lines to Your lines, and is more effective than your covering the lines with your hand, and cuing yourself.

*

**Before each rehearsal begins, you must Warm Up** both your Voice and your Body, so as to be able to bring fully-tuned "instruments" to the re-harrowing session, as described in the chapters on Voice and on Performance.

Whether it's a group warm-up, or something you do by yourself out in a corridor, or off in a corner, you Must sharpen your faculties before putting them to use. Before each rehearsal, and each performance.

\*

*Every theatre, every director, has developed over time a particular schedule of rehearsals that has proven effective, and there are of course dozens of varieties of such schedules across the country, none of which is automatically better than the others, so what I'll be describing here is a generic approach to rehearsals which can be adjusted as needed to the accepted routine at Your theatre.*

\*

Often at **the first rehearsal**, the director will introduce the entire cast, plus the Stage Manager(s), and any of the Staff who might have come to hear the play read aloud by the actual cast for the first time: designers, prop crew, publicity staff, etc. If the outline of the set has been taped on the rehearsal floor, this may be delineated and described to you, and the Costume Designer may show sketches and even swatches of material.

Then the actors, sitting around a table, or in a big circle, will read the whole play. The director may or may not make comments or suggestions between scenes, or even stopping you mid-sentence to give a direction. But you should hold off on any questions until the end of a scene, unless the director has made it clear that it's ok to interrupt the reading.

And if you have legitimate questions, tonight's the time to ask them, not two weeks into rehearsal.

The next time you meet will probably be a **Blocking Rehearsal** of the first scene, in which the director will indicate the moves the actors will make on the set. (This is described in detail in Chapter 7).

You'll write all your blocking into your script (in Pencil), and memorize it, tied to its accompanying lines, as soon as possible.

Before the entire play has been blocked, the director will call a **Working Rehearsal** for a scene or two already blocked. This will be stop-and-start to see how smoothly the movement pattern runs, or what moments need adjusting or re-blocking altogether; and the emotional levels and characterizations will be thoroughly dissected.

After several scenes have been blocked and worked, the rehearsal schedule will call for them to be **rehearsed Off Book**. Some actors roll the script up and carry it onstage in a back pocket, or tucked in a belt, so that the lines, so recently and possibly imperfectly learned, may be transferred by osmosis from the book all the way up to the mouth; sometimes this technique is effective.

*

The first time you walk out onto the rehearsal floor **without your script in hand**, whether by the director's wish or your own desire to get rid of the book and begin focusing completely on your role, **you absolutely have the right to ask to be prompted**, when you aren't sure of your next word or phrase.
**You simply need to call out loudly the word "Line!"**

When you ask for 'Line,' **stay strictly in your character and emotion, and hold your exact physical position.** If you relax your body, or neutralize your emotion, you'll ruin the continuity of the scene for yourself and for your partners.

There's no shame in calling for Line as you're getting off book; it's an accepted theatre routine, and the SM (or Prompter) is right there to toss your words to you.

Probably the director will allow this until shortly before Dress Rehearsal, but after that you're on your own.

And, in 99% of the theatre world, there is No Prompting during performances, another spur to incite you to learn your lines and cues and blocking, early and excellently.

*

As you wean yourself from your script, you'll make mistakes. And so will everyone else. That's understood. That's what rehearsals are for. That's show biz! It's no sin. **But it IS a sin if you waste everyone's time by always Apologizing for it!!!!**
You'll blow a line, or forget your blocking, or pick up the wrong prop, probably many times. So what? The playwright likely erased dozens of lines of misbegotten dialogue in the first draft of this script, and the set designer threw out a bucket of paint whose color was wrong, and the costume designer bought a bolt of cloth

that looks like mud under the stage lights.  And it's OK!   It's trial and error for all of us.

But please:  Make corrections speedily, and move on, without stealing precious rehearsal time, saying: "Oh, that's wrong. I'm sorry," every time you make a mistake.
Even worse than wasted time is how such prattle wrenches everyone out of the moment.  And vulnerable moments just being achieved in rehearsal are devilishly hard to regain after someone goofily barks: "Oh, No – Darn, I'm sorry.  Can I take that again?"
Take it again, Yes, Of Course!  But <u>with no comment</u>! Do it over, but <u>without losing concentration, or causing all your colleagues to lose theirs</u>!  Maintain the Moment!

*

**<u>Start building an ensemble from the start</u>.**  The best and happiest cast is a closely-knit ensemble, and their smooth togetherness presents the audience with a better production than ego-driven performances by several actors vying for center stage.

At the first rehearsal, greet old friends warmly, and introduce yourself to actors and stage managers whom you don't know; and if anyone ever issues an invitation to the group to go out for coffee afterwards, join in, getting to know your fellow inmates of this small "space capsule" in which you'll be working (and creating!) together for a while.
Sometimes, a cast member will host a party, or a cook-out, during the weeks of rehearsal, so the families, too, can meet each other, and enjoy the people their spouses and partners brag about at home.
If anyone asks you to help with lines, volunteer cheerfully, and hold the script as your fellow actor tries the first steps in pulling free from "the book."
Congratulate a colleague who comes off the rehearsal floor after performing a particularly fine scene – if you truly believe the work was good.  Being smarmy and praising Everything is empty. But supporting each other when you really mean it builds strong camaraderie.

\*

<u>Your director may choose to use Improvisations</u> ("<u>Improvs</u>") sometime in rehearsal. This may be to help free the emotions of one or more actors, or to insert your character into a new and different situation, to see how this person – through your body, voice and reactions – would respond in, e.g., a war zone, a class reunion, a seedy hotel.

Go for it. Listen to the guidelines the director sets, then open yourself totally to the new environment, and plunge right in.

Most such improvs last just a few minutes, but if something seems to be happening – or NOT happening – the director may let it play out for a while.

When it's over, check your body and your emotions, to see if you in fact garnered some new insight that can be carried over into the play in rehearsal – and listen very attentively to what the director feels was gained (or not).

Improvs, in the right atmosphere with the right participants, can be of great help to pinning down an elusive moment in the production. But many bring forth nothing but a short change-of-pace in rehearsal, and that can be helpful, too.

\*

<u>Rehearse fight scenes EVERY day</u>.

A fist fight, a swordfight, the knifing or bludgeoning of a character can easily cause real damage if the timing hasn't been deeply ingrained in every actor involved, as solidly as a dance number. Even if such a scene involving you isn't scheduled to be worked at every rehearsal, please take it on yourself to gather the other actor(s) during free time and work it carefully, by the numbers, in slow motion, "marking it," as dancers say, building up to full-out real-time presentation.

Then, after the play opens, the fight should be run through before each performance, to keep those moves embedded in your musculature and your subconscious, as well as in your very conscious actor's mind.

\*

In rehearsals, **impose Variety on yourself**, when you realize you're becoming a great big Bore onstage.  If you haven't experienced a Transition for a while, or changed the pitch or volume of your voice, or altered your position there on the couch, then bring yourself back to life (within the limits of the script and the style the director is seeking).  Find something in your own speeches, or someone else's, that will stimulate you into a Transition, or lower or raise your volume, or maybe just cross your legs.  Becoming too complacent with the way rehearsals are going is Dangerous!

One of my colleagues once told an improvisational class, when the last few scenes had gone nowhere: "When you realize the show is dying, Go Into Labor!"  That's a great idea for improvs, and its intent is also exactly right for a flaccid performance in rehearsal – but, while you can't actually implode the script by inducing childbirth, I suggest that you remember that phrase, and shake yourself up with a complimentary version.

\*

Speaking of which:  **If you're cast as a Pregnant woman, start observing** women in this joyous but ungainly condition whenever you see them (without being a nuisance).  You'll notice that they actually counter-balance their new belly weight by leaning backward – to avoid falling on their faces.

Probably your costume department can arrange "pregnancy padding" for you, but this prosthetic, though the size of a fetus, probably won't be as Heavy as a fetus,  so you can realistically recreate the stance of the women you've researched by occasionally wrapping a five-pound weight in a scarf tied at your midsection.

\*

Even if you have terrible eyesight, **you cannot wear your own glasses on stage,** unless the director and Costume Designer determine that your <u>character</u> wears glasses, and your frame would be a style your character would choose - - but even then it's not recommended, because the prescription lenses often reflect the stage lighting, hiding your eyes behind a couple of headlamps.

Costume glasses are most often made of plain window-glass, which doesn't reflect as badly as thick spectacles.

As a lifelong wearer of strong lenses, I'm delighted Not to take them onstage with me, because then I can actually build that 'fourth wall,' so the first few rows of the audience aren't distracting me. I can HEAR them, which helps me to wait for laughs, or pick up the pace if I'm aware of their restlessness - - but I can't See friends out front, or a nice old lady sleeping disinterestedly, so I can fully focus on my role, not distracted by anything outside the play.
And, after a decent number of rehearsals, I can find my way around the stage perfectly fine – even if not 20/20.

Going onstage without your own glasses is a big help, too, toward creating a character different from yourself. Revel in the chance to set aside these distinguishing features on your face, and move out on stage in someone else's rhythm.
Start freeing yourself from your specs as early in rehearsal as you safely can.
There's a nifty device called 'contact lenses,' too.

*

Trust your director.  It's traditional in every profession to dislike the boss, and we in the theatre are no different. Unless you're a meek little person with no ego, chances are that some evening you'll begin to feel that your director is an idiot, is directing you in the wrong way, and should be run out of town.  AVOID SUCH THOUGHTS. Douse your head in a sinkful of cold water, and wash that idea right outta your hair!

While you're having difficulty balancing everything on your plate - focusing on lines, character, emotions, unfamiliar clothing, et al - your director is juggling The Entire Cast and all their worries, as well as each of the Designers and their Crews, the Publicity Gang, the Box Office, and the fact that the air-conditioning isn't working properly.

Give this overworked leader a break, and realize that you're seeing the play from one small point of view, while the director has to envision the whole production, step by step, scene by scene, with Opening Night clearly in view - and then start believing that you're not really being directed into a train-wreck of a performance.

It would certainly help to have a talk after rehearsal, or arrange a meeting early tomorrow evening, and open up to the director about your worries – in a calm, friendly, understanding tone of voice.  And I'll bet that you'll be reassured on each of your problems, and thanked for pointing them out.

And then you can go back to rehearsal, disliking the boss as much as you like, but at least you'll believe that the show is on the right track.

*

Depending on how long the production runs, **Brush-Up Rehearsals may be necessary** after it's been open for a few weeks. As a great playwright and director is said to have written wryly to the cast of one of his productions:

"There'll be a rehearsal tomorrow morning at ten, to remove some of the 'improvements' you've added to the show."

In some theatres, these mid-run rehearsals will be supervised by the Stage Manager.

*

**Find Your Light**, beginning in Dress Rehearsal.

Unless you're playing Dracula, you've got to be seen by the audience, which means that you've got to be lit by the stage lights.  A well-designed lighting plot should insure that you'll be illuminated wherever you go on the stage, but accidents do happen.

A bulb can blow out, a lighting instrument can loosen and tilt, or perhaps the lighting designer or electrician hasn't finalized the lighting set-up - - and there you are, half-lit.

It's a good opportunity, a few days before there's an audience present, to learn how to find your light.  And it's very easy.

When you realize that you're standing in a dark spot, incline your head, or move your whole body, slowly three or four inches in each direction, until you find the right location for visibility in the ray of a spotlight.

To learn how to easily find your light, try this technique first at home, shining a lamp directly at your face. Experience how the brightness feels, the warmth, full on; then slowly move your head left or right, up or down, noting carefully the sensation of the lessening of the heat and the light. Then move your head slowly back into the light, feeling the approach of a little glimmer of the light, and then a little more (as in childhood games, you're literally "getting warmer") and finally wholly illuminated. Then, using this method when you get onto the stage and under the real lights, try to gently relocate yourself if you find you're in the dark.

But if it's a big stage, and the lights are too high for you to feel their direct warmth, pick a moment during dress rehearsal when things have stopped for a few minutes, and put your hand next to your cheek, with the open palm facing the audience. You can't see your own face out there on the stage, of course, but you Can see your flat open hand, which is an exact substitute. If the hand is fully lit, then you're ok. But if it seems a little dim, slowly move it left and right, up and down, to see if there's some more direct light nearby. If so, casually move your entire self into that better-lit location.

As Dress Rehearsal continues, you'll become more adept at feeling the stage lighting's intensity, or lack of it, on your face, without the flat-hand trick.

Now you're not only prepared to find your light under existing circumstances, but if a bulb should pop during a performance, or an instrument go astray, you'll be able to adjust yourself unobtrusively to present your fine expressive face full on to the House, in the available light.

*

## Check your troubles at the stage door.

None of us has an idyllic life in which nothing ever goes wrong, but it's a mistake to bring the problems of your family, your job or your love life into the theatre.

If there are twenty people working on the production, and each of them began expressing anger or sorrow at what's been happening at home, the emotions of the play would be overridden by the emotions of the players, and it'd be a wasted evening.

You're an actor, right?  So Act as if life is rosy, while you're rehearsing and performing, and then ask a good friend to have a cup of coffee afterward, to spill out your troubles.

*

After the play has been thoroughly rehearsed, off-Book, you're ready for Dress Rehearsal, when you can put on the real costumes and handle the real props, and play your scenes under the real lights!  But not so fast.  First comes **Technical (or Tech) Rehearsal**.

When you come to the theatre for Tech, **bring a big supply of Patience** in your backpack, because it's likely you won't have an opportunity for any real acting tonight.  The stage belongs to the Designers and their Crews, and you're incidental.

(Some theatres don't even call the Cast to Techs.  If this is true for you, skip this section and move on ahead to Dress Rehearsals.)

This is the opportunity for Director and Designers (and Producer?) to see how the scenery and costumes look under the stage lights, and to time the curtain opening and closing, the set changes, and the light, sound and music cues.

This may be just a cue-to-cue rehearsal, not bothering with the long stretches of dialogue when nothing technical changes, but if the actors are there, they'll be asked to perform the last three or four lines before each cue: telephone rings, lamp is switched on, snow starts falling outside the window, lights dim out at the end of the scene, sets are changed between scenes and/or between acts, etc.

Without the cast, it'll likely be the Assistant Stage Manager who reads the cue lines.

Tech takes a Long Time, because each cue will probably be rehearsed three or four times, to get the timing exactly right so, if you're called to be there, dip into the bagful of Patience that you brought, and smile a lot.

*

*(Each theatre has its own routine for Tech and Dress Rehearsals. Those described here are distillations of many different formats, none of which is superior to the others. Your theatre has found its own best way of approaching these very necessary, but usually very Long, rehearsals, so just overlay that procedure onto these paragraphs).*

*

After Tech comes **Dress Rehearsal** (usually shortened in speech to simply "Dress") which, depending on the timetable of your theatre, may occupy only a single evening, or two, or (it's hoped) more.

Here again, the need for your Patience is crucial, because there'll inevitably be a lot of stopping, as you and the crew orient yourselves to each other and to all the melding of Acting with Design-and-Tech elements, and, as in Tech, some of the cues will be run several times, until the whole staff is content that this is the timing that's desired.

If you have costume changes that must be accomplished quickly, within a scene, or during a very short break between scenes, please work out the procedure (by yourself or with the member of the Costume Crew who'll be helping you) as far ahead of time as you can, so your contribution to the long hours of Dress will be to complete your change(s) within the time allowed, and the rehearsal can move along without waiting for you.

Obviously, the more times the actors, and all the running crews, can play the show in full dress – costumes, make-up, scenery, props, lighting, sound, no-calling-for-line, etc – the better the continuity will flow, uninterrupted, up the Lightning Bolt, and the better prepared you'll all be for the Opening.

Be aware – Be Very Aware: <u>**The cast usually Loses their Show at the first Dress Rehearsal**</u>.

Whether you've been fortunate enough to rehearse, at least for a while, on the actual stage, or you're seeing it for the first time when you arrive for Dress, it's a certainty that meeting and absorbing all the new design and tech elements is going to take precedence over the well-crafted character and Lightning Bolt you've achieved so far.

<u>Even if you've been rehearsing on this stage for awhile</u>, and are fully acclimatized to its feeling and to the acoustics of the House, when you see yourself and everyone else in the actual costumes, amid the real scenery and carrying the real props, under the actual, very bright and very hot stage lighting, after having been used to the bare, white, low-wattage work lights, much of the rehearsed pattern (and a lot of your lines) will be driven out of your mind.  It's OK.

There'll be even more adjustments, and more discombobulation, <u>if you've rehearsed elsewhere</u>, probably in a small room with solid walls, now replaced by the open space of the wings and backstage areas surrounding the acting area, and a much higher ceiling overhead – perhaps to the limitless height of a fly loft - plus the huge void of the auditorium, stretching to a seemingly infinite scope of length and breadth and height.  This is OK, too. Everyone will adjust to the new vastness, together.

No matter how accurate the **SM** had been in laying out the floor plan of the set(s) on the rehearsal floor, and how close to reality the rehearsal furniture had been, you'll find that the spatial relationships FEEL much different.  The distance between the bar and the fireplace seems too narrow to run through, chasing the bratty kid, and the sofa too short to fling yourself onto safely.  What had felt like a small, cozy mountain cabin during rehearsals now has expanded to the size of Yankee Stadium, but contrariwise the alcove where the love scene takes place has been reduced, it feels, by half.

Though you're convinced that the pattern of performance that you had felt so good about just yesterday will never be able to come alive again in this unfamiliar space, the truth is It's All OK!   It

Can Be Done, and **has been done a billion times**, ever since the actors who had been so comfortable rehearsing the "Medea" in Euripides' back yard 2400 years ago came around the corner of the hillside and gaped at the open-air seating for 14,000 people.  Whoa!  But <u>they</u> managed the adjustment, and so can you because, though your mind may collapse at all the additions and surprises, your marrow will not – and it's from that DNA that you'll reconstitute your performance, after accepting all the beauties the designers have given you.

Instead of feeling that you may lose your show, you've just got to reinforce your concentration, and consciously and positively adopt all these new sizes and shapes and distances and weights, AS you maintain your finely-rehearsed character, your truth, your builds, your high-highs and low-lows, and some of the tricky blocking you worked on for many hours - because you know that all these new external physical trappings are going to enhance your performance, for the audience who in a day or so will be occupying those 14,000 seats (more or less).

And whether you have just One Complete Non-Stop Dress Rehearsal before you face an audience, or (ideally) several, focus every minute on and off stage to Getting Your Show Back, and reinforce your ties to the Ensemble, those artists and craftspeople from every art, melding their talents with yours to create The Play.

And, for the sweet memory of our long-ago ancestor, Thespis, the Sixth-century B.C. Greek who is celebrated as the first actor, **never, ever, refer to Rehearsal** as "<u>play-practice</u>"!!

\*

# Chapter 6

# CHARACTERIZATION

Before you've solidified any ideas about your character, and before the first rehearsal, you'll want to meet with your director for a **Character Conference**.

Take to the meeting your early thoughts about the physical and emotional make-up of the person you're going to bring to life, and listen to the director's ideas, perhaps pinning down together the exact specifics at this time, or maybe you'll both want to think some more, before settling on the final dimensions of your person.

And of course you may find that, once in rehearsal, major or minor overhauls of those 'final dimensions' may be needed. That's what rehearsals are for.

\*

To determine some traits and begin to **develop your character** even before your conference with the director, **you'll of course read your script** (the ENTIRE script, not just the pages on which you appear) **many, many times**.

Here're some of the things to look for:

- What do the other characters say about your character? How much of it is true?
- What does your character say about himself? How much of it is true?
- What does the playwright say about your character? But be careful – quite often an actor finds more and different depths and facets when approaching a character than the playwright knew had been included, so take care not to automatically believe the italicized comments the author has inserted into the script, some of which are based on the actor who originated the role, perhaps many years and three continents distant.

*(I apologize for using here the old-fashioned masculine-gendered pronouns – "He, Him, and His" – when referring to your character, but I'll switch to feminine pronouns in upcoming examples.)*

- What does he want?  What drives him through the play?
- Who is he? What was his early life like, and his parents?
- How Intelligent is he, and what kind of Education? (They're different things.)
- What is the physical and emotional environment he lives in now, and how has he adapted to it – or not?
- What does he look like?  What's his age – both chronological AND emotional?
    > Height and Weight
    > Hair style and upkeep
    > Facial hair or Street make-up
    > Clothes, how they look and how they're worn
    > Voice – pitch and pace
    > Dialect? Regional American, Foreign?

*

As you make all those choices, you'll also be deciding on your character's basic **Rhythm**.  **This is how she moves through life, every day**, regardless of how she feels or what stimuli hit her, moment by moment.  Your decisions about her rhythm will begin with "Fast" or "Slow," and then touch base with the variations therein, as Speedy, Rapid-Fire, Fleet-footed, Brisk, Nimble, etc. . . . or. . . . . Languid, Painstaking, Deliberate, Foot-dragging, Poky, etc. This is who she is, how she moves, whether happy or sad, <u>always</u>.

Then: The **Tempo** of the character **encompasses the moment-by-moment Changes** (Transitions) **within** her Rhythm, throughout the play, caused by the stimuli tossed at her: Falling in love, receiving a threatening letter, learning that she has a horrible disease, or, less intense: getting a phone call from a friend, stubbing her toe, smelling dinner cooking in the kitchen.

As you're tracing this **Rhythm/Tempo** pattern of your character through the script and into rehearsal, never lose sight of the fact that <u>her Rhythm never changes</u>.  Yes, <u>the Tempo changes frequently</u>, generally on a Transition, but always **Within** <u>her single Rhythm</u>.

Paul, a character with a "Brisk" rhythm, for instance, picks up a baby, <u>tenderly and gently</u>, but <u>Still Brisk</u>.

Joan, a character with a "Languid" Rhythm, reacts with <u>fear</u> when she realizes there's a fire in the house, and runs into the back yard, <u>terrified</u>.  But her languid Rhythm will <u>never</u> approach the briskness of Paul's.      And vice versa.

Paul's brusque nature is softened by the baby, and Joan's languor is speeded up by the impending fire, but those <u>Tempo changes must Never cause them to become someone else, to lose their absolutely consistent character Rhythms</u>.

*

**<u>Learn what your own "isms" are, and work to Replace them</u>** with what you determine the Character's "isms" to be.  Do you tend (e.g.) to lick your lips a lot? or play with your hair?  or twist the ring on your finger?  or continually cross and recross your legs, when sitting? Slump your shoulders?

Check yourself and find out! Your physical character in the play should not be based on <u>your</u> mannerisms, so create some that are totally Different From Yours, based on what you've decided about your role.

Perhaps she pats down her hair a lot, or he sits with one foot resting on the other, or usually stands fully erect, as if suspended by a string.  Good.  Incorporate the "isms" that you choose, and divest yourself of your own, when you're onstage or in rehearsal.

*

For you, as for many actors, creating an onstage character perhaps can be aided by **using a Prototype**, i.e. someone whose appearance, voice and/or Rhythm are similar to the desired character in the play, but different from you yourself.

Decide on the traits that you need to adopt (purposeful stance, e.g., or round, caressing vowels, or piercing eye contact, etc.) and <u>select and observe someone who has them</u>; then put that person into action in your imagination, and recreate those traits when working on your script at home – and carry your prototype into rehearsal, in your growing personification, as you sharpen and perfect your character, day by day.

Perhaps you'll want <u>several</u> prototypes – one for body, one for voice, one for a distinctive walk, for example.

It's wise to select as prototypes people you see frequently, so you have a very strong, current and nearby image in your mind. But be careful not to become a stalker.

Never try to imitate the work of <u>another actor</u>, neither someone in your group nor a famous movie star, for that becomes a copy of a copy, and loses great hunks of verisimilitude with each trip to the mental photocopy machine. Draw from <u>life</u>, not from other performers.

*

Beyond finding the opportunity to look carefully - and discreetly - at your prototype(s), **keep looking every day for interesting characteristics** shown by <u>others</u>, too. Look for mannerisms and stances and walks and hairstyles and ways of handling props, and then file the images away for possible use for a character, or even for just a moment, in a future performance.

The way someone tucks his thumbs in his belt, or chews on the end of a strand of hair, or scissors her legs when she sashays across the room, or hangs a sweater over just one shoulder, appearing ultra-casual or perhaps foolish.

The use of a prototype, and your ever-watchful eye for useable traits, are parts of one of the most necessary aspects of actor-training, which should energize you every day for as long as you live: **OBSERVATION of the world around you**.

When my children were very young and we'd go for a walk on the campus where I taught, they'd often point out to me things of beauty or novelty that I'd never noticed: architectural tchotchkes on some of the decades-old buildings, a bird's nest in a tree, a misspelled word on a permanent sign, the juxtaposition of a decorative metal lantern with the faded brick behind it.  Their unsophisticated but dead-on discoveries put me to shame, since in my usual hurried dashes from building to building I was too (needlessly) preoccupied to take notice – to Observe – the wonderfulness available at every hand.

Let this innocence of youth instruct us, no matter how busy our days, or cluttered our minds, to keep our eyes and our minds open.  I urge you to look higher than the ground-level stores and office buildings you pass every day, to see what interesting gimcracks were designed or later added up there; and focus on the pattern of the sidewalk lay-out, and the trees and plantings in the park; and of course zero in on the People who cross your vision, male and female, young and old, staid and unconventional.

*

As indicated at the top of this Chapter, **your character may LIE**, or exaggerate, or joke about a serious subject - **find out when and where**, and how you'd like to deal with this bending of the truth.

Such probing can also save you from embarrassment.  In a light American comedy a young woman, viewing the very funny events that have brought absolute chaos to her normally normal family, says: "Well, to top it all off, I probably should announce that I'm having a baby!"  She's kidding, she's being sarcastic, but you can see how taking this line as gospel truth would distort the play. Get real!  Read between the lines. Find the truth.

*

Some actors find that **working with Animal Images** helps create the physical and/or vocal characteristics of the person they're presenting.

Some playwrights make this easy.  Ben Jonson in his "Volpone," for instance, has named the title character for the Italian word for "fox," and the cast includes Mosca (the horsefly, or parasite), Corvino (the raven), Colomba (the dove), and Leone, the lion.

But rarely will a playwright <u>hand you</u> such an animal image, and anyway it's more fun and more creative to find your own.  Is your character shy and retiring, like a Mouse?  Or heavyset and galumphing, like a Walrus?  Or twittery and unable to sit still, like a Hummingbird?  Give it a try.  It doesn't work for every actor, but when it does it can be a terrific aid.

*

Sometimes in resident companies, community theatres, summer theatres or schools, young people are cast as old people.  Seeking Prototypes, and sensitivities toward the elderly, a successful characterization can definitely be accomplished.

But: **Avoid the caricature "Old-man Walk,"** shuffling along as if your shoes are glued to the floor, **and the "Old-woman Talk,"** gumming the words and smacking your lips like a chimpanzee.

Many young actors consider anyone over 35 to be Old, and anyone over 50 to be Ancient, so they grab a cane or thick spectacles and wobble across the stage, speaking in the voice of a mummified driveller.  No!  Get to know or closely observe middle-aged and older people, and learn what has <u>really</u> happened to their joints, their centers of gravity, their jaws and lips, and at what approximate age.

In discussing a particular play, a twenty-year-old actress found great hilarity in a male character referring to his "girl-friend."  "He's over 50," she chortled.  "Who's he kidding??!!"  Ah, young lady, time will tell you who's kidding whom.

*

**Make Exposition work for you**.  It's a sad and simple fact that much of the dialogue in the early moments of the play, and the early moments following each character's first entrance, is purely Exposition - a plot device to give the audience the information they have to know in order to understand what's happening, and going to happen, in the development of the storyline.

To their discredit, many actors mindlessly do just that - give Basic Information in a thankless delivery of cold facts. And bore the pants off the audience.

**Think of it like this:  Your first few minutes on stage are vitally important**, if you will use that expository dialogue to show the audience Who This Person Is, by displaying specific personality traits; and How You Feel about the info you're sharing, so, as they're learning about you, they're learning more of the background of the plot, and your position in the story that's starting to unfold.

To accomplish this, enter armed with full stage energy and a firm grasp of your character, deeply entrenched in the style of the play, thereby assuring the spectators that they're going to be very comfortable, spending the evening with you.

Sure, this is asking you to be egotistic, because it takes a boatload of ego to stand in front of several hundred people, saying, intrinsically, "Look at Me!" - but this is the sort of egotism that every actor must have to even audition, and then to perform - - - and your task then is to Channel that egotism, to be totally in keeping with the character and the play, not stealing focus or scenes, not breaking character, but underline presenting that character in full, confident and stageworthy.

If you're alone on stage at the beginning of the action, it gives you a wonderful chance to establish your character clearly from the very outset.  If the director will allow you, **create some believable stage business before you speak**, which exemplifies your character. If it's a comedy, some character-driven comedic business may garner some laughs for you and for the production, which is a marvelous way to start the show – and Your portion of the show.

This "action before dialogue" can be helpful when*ever* your first entrance occurs in the play, to set up Who You Are, and How Your Character fits into the plot.

The way you take off your hat or coat, check the answering machine, straighten a sofa pillow, check yourself in the mirror, put a pan onto the stove, select a book from a shelf - - - Everything you say and do on stage enhances – or diminishes – the solidity of your character; <u>just always be sure that the real You is Not showing through</u>.

*

# Chapter 7

# BLOCKING

**Blocking is every movement, and every piece of business, seen on stage**: Crossing to the window, pouring a drink, sitting down, taking a handkerchief from your pocket, hitting, kissing, standing, writing, coughing, turning, etc. The director will block each scene, and may encourage you to initiate moves that you feel are called for by the character, the emotion and the situation. When the director is satisfied with a piece of blocking, you'll write it into your script - always in Pencil, for as rehearsals proceed, the blocking may change. (Beware the blocking already printed there, for that came from another production on another set, with another director, possibly many years ago.)

There is rarely enough white space in scripts for you to write your blocking in full sentences, so use lots of abbreviations. "X" for Cross, "DL" for Down Left, etc.

**Blocking is character in motion.**
Every move you make, and the way you handle each prop, is a Physical Expression of your Character. This is useful to you, twice: The way you interpret the person you're playing influences the way you move. AND: The way you move adds more levels in communicating the depth of your character to the audience.

**So every movement is of far more importance** than merely transporting you to a new spot on stage, blowing your nose, or finishing that sandwich. As discussed in the previous chapter, it personifies your character.

*

**A move from one location to another is called a Cross.**
"Cleopatra crosses to the throne;" "Othello crosses from UL to DR in a rage;" "Jennifer, please cross to the left end of the sofa, but hold off on sitting down until your next line."

*

**A Vector** is the invisible line along which an actor walks from one place to another.

When you cross from a chair to the fireplace, say, and then shortly cross back again, <u>along the same vector</u>, it's called '<u>**wearing a hole in the carpet**</u>,' and the audience calls it 'Boring!' for it kills their focus and attention.

**AND:** Just as you avoid repeating that same crossing-back-and-forth, please also refrain from sitting on the same bench where you sat few minutes ago with the same leg crossed, or perching on the back of the sofa atop the same cushion, or slipping your left hand <u>again</u> into your jacket pocket, as you place your right foot <u>again</u> on the first step of the staircase; or leaning against the same side of the French doors, or cave opening, or oak tree, etc.  Variety is the spice of theatre!  Resist repetition!

*

There are **only Two Kinds of Moves on stage – Toward something or Away from something**.  That's all.  <u>Wandering is not acceptable, nor is Backing Up</u> (unless you're being chased by a lion – or, as in that wonderful Shakespearean stage direction in "A Winter's Tale": "Exit, pursued by a bear.")

When you move away from something or someone, simply turn away and walk or run <u>forward</u>. Walking backwards can result in an embarrassing fall.

And then please be sure you **end each cross At a tangible object** – a piece of furniture, a wall, or another person.  Finding yourself in a big open space can be very lonely, unless you're preparing to present a soliloquy, and not always then.

In "The Gin Game," which had practically nothing on stage except a card table, two chairs, and empty spaces, the actor Hume Cronyn at one point threw a folded newspaper onto the floor ten feet away, Down Center, and then a few minutes later crossed down to the paper.  He had in effect created his Own vector, ending at that sort-of-solid object, so the audience wasn't made ill at ease by the sight of him isolated in space.

*

A chair, table or sofa is a logical end point for a Vector, but when you get there please <u>let the audience see you</u>. **If you "feature the furniture"** i.e. stand behind a piece of furniture so it hides much of your body**, the audience will wonder what in the world you're doing back there,** or, worse, they'll forget about you altogether.

The same thing happens **if you Cross Behind (Upstage of) another Standing actor.  You'll disappear momentarily,** and that's not in your best interest - unless you're blocked to strangle or stab that actor.  Work it out with the director so that, instead, you may cross Below such a standing actor.

Years ago, I was with a professional production in which the leading man one night during a long speech crossed above the actress playing the maid, stopped directly upstage of her and, never changing the tempo of his speech, unzipped the back of her dress just far enough to unsnap her bra, unbeknownst to anyone but her, and continued crossing the stage, convinced he was the funniest guy in town.  Vile!

So, Yes, it's a good idea not to <u>let anyone</u> Cross Behind <u>you</u>, either!

*

Every performance presents to the audience many thousands of stage pictures, with the proscenium arch as an actual picture frame.  Every time you move your arm, much less stand on your head, **you're changing the stage picture**, and must make the exact move that the "painter" of this picture has asked for – the director, who can see what you cannot see: the entire stage, every second.  Part of directing is calling for specific adjustments to the "picture" to further the action, and the style, of your play.

But if you realize that you've been directed into making a repetitive move, as in "wearing a hole in the carpet," you can follow directions and still save yourself by <u>varying the blocking slightly</u>, e.g. by pausing for a few seconds halfway along the Vector, or sitting on the <u>edge</u> of the chair, or moving <u>a few feet further than before</u> along the sofa, fireplace or crenellated castle wall.

This also applies if you're directed to **Rise from a chair, Cross to another chair, and then Sit down again as soon as you reach the new location.  This will obviously look to the audience as a move Blocked by the director,** not flowing naturally from the character.  If the director insists on it, then go on and rise, make the cross, but DELAY sitting for a line or two - - and I'll bet the director will see that this more believable timing is an improvement.

*

Many an actor, if asked "Why did you cross to the cellar door on that line?" will reply brightly:  "Because the director told me to."

Well, No. Wrong Answer.  Sure, that was the Original reason, but now **it's up to you to Justify the cross** within the context of your character at that moment in the play.  Really - Why ARE you crossing?  Are you going Toward the cellar, or Away from the angry woman?  And if you can't find a reason, you must talk it over with the director, who'll help you pin down the motivation.  (But how much more satisfying if you can discover, and create, motivation for yourself. And Yes, something must spur that move.)

I don't want to foment friction between you and your director, but it's perfectly permissible for you, in similar situations, to say:  "Y'know, it doesn't feel right to cross yet; I think I ought to stay close to her, and fight against her anger."

In other words, Stay Put Till You HAVE To Move – until your Gut tells you to.

Oh, Boy, we're getting into a ticklish area here, much of which depends on your grasp of your character, your director's trust of that grasp, and how well you two work together.  I don't want to cause problems, but as both an actor and a director, I believe that a good actor who's been working hard at the role knows as much (or more) about the character's inner life as the director does, deep into rehearsal.

But I'll stop here.  As Alfred P. Doolittle said, "I put it to ya, and I leave it to ya."

*

    <u>Avoid creating a straight line as you stand next to several other actors,</u> unless the director wants that unreal effect.  When you realize that this uninteresting, unnatural line has been created, take a step forward, or back, or sideways, to restore a pleasing <u>unevenness</u> to the stage picture.

    Too, <u>be careful not to perform the same Movement as anyone else on stage</u> - sitting at same time, drinking in tandem, etc. It's tedious, and looks manufactured.

    Nor <u>assume the same Position as anyone else on stage</u> - legs crossed, or arms folded, or hands on hips, etc.

    Thus: <u>if someone echoes Your position, gently transition yourself into another</u>.

    These parallel visuals might cause unwanted laughter out front, so avoid them - UNLESS such a comic effect is sought.

    Yes, every time you take a step or alter the position of any part of your body, you're creating a new Stage Picture. So make sure it <u>is</u> a new one, and that your move is a genuine move, realistically motivated.

*

    <u>If you stand directly in front of a chair, the audience will be expecting you to sit</u>.  If you continue to stand there, and stand there, and stand there, they'll be unconsciously using their body language to urge you to "Sit Down, for Pete's sake!!" and that'll badly interrupt their concentration.  So sit already, or move your body into a new position, away from the center of the chair, not forecasting a subsidence.

    A line or two before you're blocked to sit, be sure that you've checked out the exact position of the chair or sofa (unobtrusively) so you can <u>sit without having to look at the seat first</u> - which would break your, and the audience's, concentration.  Feel it with the back of your leg, and then sit with confidence in one fluid motion.  No peeking.

This strong, positive Sit also prevents you from manifesting the most ungraceful move seen on any stage, the **Prehensile Butt Grab**, in which the actor gets within a foot or so of the chair and starts crouching down and backing up, seemingly trying to Reach Out with his backside to find the furniture and glom onto it. Most inelegant. Ascertain that the seat is there, and then smoothly seat your seat onto it.

*

In the Olden Days, actors executed what I now call **"Miss Galflong's Flat Turn**, "so the audience can always see your pretty face!" And it's so wrong, and so stagy.

The idea was that, when you turned, you did so <u>by never showing your back</u> to the House. You may work for a director who asks for this, so be prepared. This is it:

Let's say you're talking to your grandfather, who's in a chair six feet to your Left. The director asks that, as you talk, you cross toward him, then below him, and then <u>beyond</u> him - and then turn back to face him, as you finish talking.

To accomplish this, Miss Galflong demands that your face be always open to the audience so that, after you've gone past your dear old Gramp, <u>you turn to your Right, which has you now facing the audience straight on, and continue turning Right, which now, finally, brings you face-to-face with the dear old guy</u> - - but via the Long Way, Wrong Way, Around, 180 full degrees. Arggggh!!

You see how un-real such a turn is, and though, Yes, you're staying Open, you look wrong-footed and very artificial, revolving as no human being really turns. So:

Defying Miss Galflong, I suggest this:

**Move Naturally** (even though Yes, your face will be upstage for 1½ seconds, mid-turn) by focusing your eyes on the eyes of the actor playing Grandfather, all during your cross to him. Keep that eye contact as you cross below him, and, when you get beyond him, gently turn to your left, <u>and come to a stop, fully open to the House,</u> in a ¾ position <u>facing Grandfather, **having never broken eye contact with him**</u>.

All right, so the audience has fleetingly glimpsed your back! Who Cares? You have their attention, for You're speaking and You're moving, and your tight eye contact with the other actor makes a strong and unyielding bid for full audience focus, and you've avoided the old-fashioned, unnatural Flat Turn.

Sorry, Miss Galflong.

\*

**The Side-step** might work very well in a dance number, but in a realistic play it **pulls the audience right out of their belief**. Instead of sidling toward your wife with your toes always facing the audience, Turn toward her and then walk straight at her, like a human being, for goodness' sake!

\*

**When you cross while speaking, time your dialogue With the cross**, so you finish the line **as** you finish the cross, i.e., stop Walking and stop Talking at the same time.

If your line ends two steps before the end of the cross, it causes you to sneak into the new position in dead silence, since the actor with the next line isn't going to speak while focus is still on a moving actor - you.

Using this same technique, **Give yourself a clean exit**. Time your last line to end at the instant you disappear through the door (or into the woods, etc.). If you complete the line four feet before you reach the exit, or get there too quickly, you'll find yourself with proverbial egg on your face, instead of (maybe) generating a solid appreciative applause to accompany you into the darkened wings.

\*

**Use your shoulder to hide things from other characters**, but not from the audience. If you swing your shoulder around so it blocks the vision of another actor as you put the poison in the drink, or squeeze the hand of your secret lover, the audience will understand that they've got knowledge the other characters in the play haven't, and they'll feel privileged, and can follow the plot with more savvy.

*

"Oh, Sandy **never does the same thing once.**"  This was told me by a Broadway actor about one of his co-stars.   During rehearsal, it's fine – in fact it's excellent – for you to search for and offer to your director new and different movements and pieces of business that best express your character and emotion, but by the time you get into Dress Rehearsal, and certainly into Performances - for the sake of the rest of the cast – and your own artistic discipline - you'd better have set a pattern and kept to it.

*

If you accidentally place yourself further upstage than another actor, forcing her to turn away from the audience to look at and speak to you, **this is an unforgivable sin called "Upstaging."** **Avoid It.**

Just as in skiing and driving a car, **the responsibility for safety lies with the person Behind** (in our case, Upstage).  TAKE that responsibility, so you aren't doing dirt to your colleagues by unthinkingly upstaging them.

And certainly never <u>Deliberately</u> upstage anyone.  Too often, mischievous Actor A begins sneaking just a little bit more upstage than Actor B, causing B to look away from the audience, or to move up a little to maintain audience visibility, which A takes as a challenge to move further up, starting a visible, regrettable dual in one-upmanship (or one-upstagemanship!) until both A and B are pressed against the back wall of the stage, each trying to win the dubious crown of farthest-upstage, and least-gracious actor in town.

By the same rule, **you shouldn't upstage yourSELF**!  Always have at least one eye, if not both, looking below (i.e. Downstage of) the proscenium arch.  This keeps your expressive face always within the audience's view.

You can help achieve this by standing in what's called **the ¾ position** – i.e. with the Upstage foot forward, and the downstage foot at a right angle to it, in a T-shape almost like ballet's Third Position. This keeps the Magic Triangle always fully in view of the audience -

an invisible line from your bellybutton to one shoulder, straight across to the other shoulder and back down to your navel - from where much of your emotion is projected.

This ¾ position has the additional benefit of allowing you **to speak straight across the toes of either foot,** using each foot as a directional arrow focusing your voice toward other actors.  Then: When it comes time to speak to an actor who is Not aligned with one of your feet, you confidently rotate your body, pivoting on the balls of both feet as you start to speak, so one foot is newly pointing at the person you're addressing – and you're not having to raise your feet from the floor, or twist your body like a corkscrew, or demonstrate your <u>Barbie-doll Waist</u>, flexible and supple, but of negative use on stage.

And you'll have again attained **the ideal position, speaking across your toes**.

*

While you're being a polite and cooperative colleague, as you avoid upstaging anyone, **be careful not to let yourself be Covered** by a Downstage actor slipping absentmindedly, or intentionally, between you and the audience – making you invisible. If someone does this, theatre law makes it permissible for you to topple this scoundrel into the orchestra pit.

*

**Little, small, tiny steps should be used rarely**, and then only as specific character traits, or to illustrate humongous fear.

Ordinarily, when you cross the stage, **take full strides,** as part of your manifestation of Actor's Energy.  And when you stop at the end of your cross, bring both feet strongly and positively into the modified T-position.  If you stop smartly with the leading foot, but then dragggggg the trailing foot to a delayed stop, any strength the cross has manifested for your character will be lost, in this weak and uncertain finish.

<u>Snap</u> that trailing foot into place, and stand strong and tall.

*

**If one of your Crosses takes you up onto a Platform** - which serves on the set as a porch, a step adjacent to the front door, the bottom of a flight of stairs, or any other of the practical uses of platforms to vary the relative heights of the actors, positioned across the stage - be very careful.  Platforms are often built onto castors (wheels) for easy set-changing so, when you step onto one, **plant your weight Downward**, so you're tightening the castors to the floor – and not Across the platform, which is liable to activate the castors, sending the platform scurrying into the Wings, taking you unwillingly with it.

*

**Use Down Center (D.C.) selectively**, perhaps once in the entire play, for a very important speech – because it's such a forceful, attention-grabbing position, and usually free of any furniture or set pieces, so you're naked and vulnerable and had BETTER have some strong dialogue and/or emotion to justify your being there.

If the director blocks you to cross D.C. and stop, when you haven't any such powerful reason to be there, help yourself out by stopping <u>short</u>, at D.L.C., or D.R.C. – and the director will, we hope, realize that you've chosen a better position.

*

A good way to **strengthen a Transition is by making a physical move** at the moment you have left the old emotion behind, and are stepping confidently into the new emotion.

The sort of movement to identify a Transition might be to simply raise your head understandingly as the new emotion starts to wash over you, or set down your drinking glass, or turn to the window, or stop in the midst of closing a door.  Clear, believable, easy actions, or <u>cessation</u> of actions, are nifty tools for an actor.

**Yes, STOPPING a physical action is a great emotional statement.**  When another character enters suddenly, or says something unexpectedly, a clear sign to the audience that you've been affected by it is suddenly stopping, abruptly interrupting whatever you've been doing – pouring a drink, walking across the stage, stacking logs in the fireplace.  Stopping dead.  The audience certainly realizes that Something has happened.

And it's a great boost to a Transition.

\*

**Sitting or lying on the floor** can be an interesting way to vary your blocking – and may look great in the rehearsal room.  But when you move onto the actual stage, check how low the first couple of rows of seats are, relative to the height of the stage - and adjust the height of your head proportionately so everyone in the entire House can still see you.

Scope this out extra carefully if you're playing in an **arena theatre,** where the first row is often on the same level as the stage, and therefore people in those seats are the only ones who can see you, supine on the hearth rug. Hold your head high, or you'll become a disembodied voice to the rest of the audience.

\*

When you're blocked to switch on, or off, a light, the chances are that the switch on the wall or on the lamp isn't connected to Anything, but that the electrician sitting offstage at the switchboard will actually control the dousing or the illuminating of a lamp or sconce or ceiling light, along with the accompanying stage lighting.

Your responsibility is to **put your finger(s) onto the switch without covering it with your body,** so the stage manager or the lighting crew can clearly see your action, and cause the lights to change.  And of course you must keep your finger(s) in place until the cue has been completed.

\*

If you're serving someone a meal or a drink, **serve from UPSTAGE of the patron,** so as not to cover that actor, nor upstage yourself.

\*

Ah, for the bad old days when people smoked **cigarettes!** Now, of course, we realize they're lethal - - but at one time they **provided dozens of possible bits of business** and timing, and helped establish character.

And on Arena or Thrust Stages, where playing too long with your back to a segment of the audience can frustrate those patrons who can't see your face or hear you too well, the dictum was: Put too few ashtrays on the set, so that smoking actors would have to keep changing positions to tap or extinguish their cigarettes, thus opening themselves up to another quadrant of the audience.

Now that some period television shows are restoring smoking into the action, they've found that **"herbal cigarettes"** look like the real thing, without endangering anyone. If your production of "Private Lives" or "The Front Page" utilizes these substitute "cancer sticks," here're a couple of suggestions:

Reaching out to touch your lover with a cigarette in that hand is pretty gauche, though the eccentric actress Tallulah Bankhead was celebrated for embracing her leading man, and then, in the embrace, taking a puff of the cigarette held in the hand that was encircling his neck.  There are few Tallulahs in the world, though, so keep your cigarette (and its smoke) away from your colleagues, on stage and off.
Lighting a cigarette during someone else's line is grounds for pitching you through the nearest window.

If you're unfamiliar with smoking, you can't fake it by taking a puff, holding it in your mouth for a few seconds, and then expelling it in one big explosive exhale.  Uh-Uh.  The ex-smokers in the audience will lose focus on the scene while guffawing at this clumsy imitation.  Work on the technique at home, so you look as proficient as your worldly-wise and foolhardy character.

*

**To threaten a person, you've got to get close,** whether verbally or with a gun or baseball bat.  If the bad guy stands halfway across the stage, he can't very well intimidate the little guy, for all the airspace in the world surrounds them both, notifying us in the audience that no one is really in danger.

<u>Gradually work yourself closer and closer to your quarry</u>, <u>through the whole length</u> of your line, or during the duologue between you.  If you expend your emotional force with one long quick move, you'll have no ammunition left, as you stand there, already face-to-face, with twenty impotent words remaining to be said, dribbling down your chin.

*

<u>Kissing must look to the audience as passionate as the script</u> <u>dictates, but must actually for the actors be as mundane and</u> <u>workaday as eating mashed potatoes in a dinner scene</u>.

Some theatres (and some actors) prefer to <u>avoid</u> actual mouth-to-mouth contact by turning both heads upstage, as soon as the faces get close to each other, with the director in rehearsal noodging them into a position that looks amatory from out front, but doesn't embarrass (or arouse) either of the actors or either of the watching real-life spouses.

But come on, folks, if this bit of blocking is approached professionally, the kiss can look real from Any angle and can engage the audience as it should at this point in the play which, like the kiss, is about the relationship of the <u>two Characters</u> – Not the actors who are playing them.  Get over it.

The director will choreograph the love scene as carefully and as schematically as a dance movement, directing you both into the embrace in a realistic manner, and then into the kiss (<u>Mouths Kept</u> <u>Closed, always, of course</u>.)
The passion, to the degree called for in the plot, can be intensified by gently moving the heads during the kiss, and by having each actor's hands, as they grip the partner's shoulders or back, move around slowly, increasing their hold on each other.

Especially if either actor is uneasy about the kiss, you should begin rehearsing it early in the rehearsal period, and in slow, unthreatening stages, until everyone does, in fact, rightfully treat it like any other piece of stage business.

If the love scene as written, or as directed, must go Beyond a kiss, then attention to the details described above must be even more stringently adhered to.

(And, truly, a stage kiss that gets even slightly out of hand can naturally affect the emotional control of the actors and seriously affect their timing, and that's plainly Wrong, because if you lose touch with what you're doing, you may be human, but you're no artist.)

*

### Crying on stage can be very tricky, and must be approached with craftsmanship.

Some actors can bring forth real tears easily, but this might not be as helpful as it sounds.  Certainly tears are useful and a plus in a movie, because that's a naturalistic art form, presented literally as photographic realism in which the audience expects and appreciates car crashes, explosions, running water in the tub, fire in the fireplace, falling buildings in a Martian attack, real blood - - - - and the sight of real tears emerging from the heroine's eyes and rolling down her face.

BUT:  On stage, we're presenting Life as an Art Form, and too much Naturalism can distract from the ever-rising Lightning Bolt.  No matter how completely the audience has left their disbelief behind in the lobby, or how magically the production has captured their attention and their empathy, there's still a part of every mind that KNOWS it's in a theatre, looking at open-sided scenery and actors playing roles - so that when "rain" or "snow" begins to fall outside the window, many will find themselves wrenched away from their emotional participation, wondering how that effect was technically created. . . . and this same impulse to pull free from the involvement of the play can be triggered by those little salty drops cascading down a face.

Once, when I was having dinner with the president of the college where I taught, he leaned over to me and asked, "Have you seen John Gielgud in the play 'Home'?"  "Oh, yes," I replied, expecting a lively conversation on the play as a metaphor for the economic failures of Great Britain.  "Tell me," he said, "how did he make himself cry in the second act?"  Indeed!  Even intelligent people who've attended the theatre all their lives are fascinated by "How did he cry??" and that's <u>not</u> what the play was about.

So my recommendation is: **<u>REAL WEEPING - ACTUAL TEARS – WILL DISTANCE YOUR AUDIENCE, rather than DRAWING THEM CLOSER</u>**.  So even if you're proud of your ability to let pour the waterworks on cue, I submit that you'll just distract the audience away from what is probably one of the more important moments of the play.

Here's what I suggest you do:

As with every aspect of recreating life on the stage, you'll observe actual crying (your own and other people's) when you see it in life, and mark carefully the snuffles of the nose, and the vibrations of the sounds made on the exhale (Oh-oh-oh-oh-oh) and the inhale (UhUhUh) and other half-formed words carrying the anguish.  And then in the quiet of your room you'll rehearse and rehearse, recreating these sounds, and the crumpling of the face, and the body's turning-in on itself, so you'll be able to recreate the act of crying, when next it's needed - but dryly.

Add to this the <u>HIDING</u> of your eyes from the audience, so no one will grumble to his wife, "I can't see any tears," which is worse than "Where did those tears come from?"  Holding a wavering hand over your eyes, or burying your face in a pillow, is not only a common accompaniment of weeping in the real world, but it'll shield your dry eyes from the audience.

Your emotional approach to acting may suggest here that you imagine a best friend in the hospital, or the death of a childhood dog, or some other irreparable assault on your equilibrium.  Fine; I'll endorse ANY Internal trigger as long as it doesn't cause your make-up to run down your face, but what I've just described is the External way to present this weepy moment safely to a waiting audience.

The last, very important part of whatever weeping technique you use is:  **Keep your voice production CLEAR and UNOBSTRUCTED**.  Wailing or sobbing must SUPPORT, not OBSCURE, the dialogue of the play, so work carefully to keep the vibrato and the sounds of hopelessness streaming through your mouth, but at the same time <u>articulate every word</u> that the playwright has given you.  Too many weepy scenes have abandoned all intelligible words into the Waaaaaaahhhh of the uncontrolled actor.  No. We want the sorrow, but we want the necessary accompanying dialogue articulated, also.

*

Similarly, <u>there's nothing worse than a Phony Laugh on stage</u>.  The best laughter is the real kind, brought from the recesses of your gut, tickled out of you by something that <u>really makes you laugh</u>, every time you think of it:

The punch line of a favorite joke, or the image of an overly-righteous public figure after a pie has hit him in the face, or whatever in your own personal sense of humor generates laughter.

If none of these stimuli works for you consistently, the always-faithful technical approach is quite simple:

Working at home, roll these syllables sequentially around in your mouth:  "HaHa, HeHe, HoHo," (Yeah, the old cliché is based on truth!) again and again...and as you build your way into the repetition, start actively flapping your uvula, and then leave the "H"s off the words ("ah ah, ee ee, oh oh," etc) and get your face and your whole body into the act, vibrating with the rhythms of the coruscating vowels – and THEN dredge up a visual of a haughty person dropping through a trap door – or whatever image will give a personal true stimulus to your "Ha"s and "He"s, "Ah"s and "Ee"s.  Or just your "Oo"s.

After you've tried this exercise a few times, you'll find which of these sounds works best for you – to give a representation of a real laugh. Everyone's different; find your own key to believable yuks, and abandon the others.

*

**When you're alone on stage, eat it up!  Enjoy it!**  All eyes are on you, so, without nullifying the plot or the style of your show, do whatever business you're directed to do, including just sitting and waiting for the phone to ring, or another character to enter, with full actor's energy, showing your character traits and your emotion. Picking up a magazine, pouring a cup of coffee, looking out the window can be a wishy-washy piece of homely activity, or it can carry forward the play (and you).

Are you (in character) entitled to that cup of coffee?  What do you see out that window?  Who's going to be making that phone call? Make every moment you're out there alone Count!

And if it's a Comedy, well, can you and your director create some terrific character-driven comic business for that solo time?

*

Most directors will encourage or accept **suggestions from the actors**, of New blocking, or changes in blocking, well into the rehearsal period, but if you change your blocking without asking the director, you risk being stepped on in the physical confusion that ensues, or being unceremoniously dumped off the apron by the cast members whose own blocking has been fouled up by your thoughtlessness.

*

Sight (or "Site") lines are invisible lines stretching along both sides of the stage, beyond which, left and right, you move out of sight of some members of the audience.  During onstage rehearsals, cast a glance out into the house, to see the furthermost seats on each side, and then be very **careful not to drift so far to either side of the stage as to disappear** from the eyes of the people who'll be occupying those seats during performances.

*

# Chapter 8

# Taking Control of your Body

Just as an athlete, **an actor must achieve and maintain good physical condition**. You're going to be putting in long hours, often continually on your feet, and sometimes this will be asked of you after a full stint at your "day job" or school, or managing a family, and your body must be ready for such a long haul, and primed for quick responses and adjustments.

Set yourself a rigorous exercise regimen at a gym or at home, even before auditions, and keep it up all the way through rehearsals and performances.

Good Mental and Psychological condition is also demanded. (See "Check your troubles at the stage door," in Chapter 5.)

\*

**Take charge of every part of Your Body, and never let it take charge of you.**

If you're not always alert while you're onstage, your body will try to take command, and betray you in a hundred different ways, such as twiddling or drumming your fingers, licking or chewing on your lips, swinging your foot when your legs are crossed, shifting your weight from foot to foot while standing, smiling inanely in a dramatic scene, unconsciously clenching your hands, and other inappropriate and distracting sights and sounds, which announce the fact that you're out of control – or at least not In control.

To help sharpen that alertness, try to **develop the ability to always "see" every physical aspect of yourself**, as if you were an audience member - to check to be sure you're moving in character at all times, and wearing your costume properly, and not making random, uncontrolled movements, which could betray your nervousness or inattention, and steal focus. This is called the **Outside Eye**.

A first-rate actress once told me she understood this concept very well, in her real life: "Without looking down, I know exactly how much cleavage I'm showing." I had to agree that that indeed was a perfect example of the Outside Eye.

Experiment with your own Outside Eye right now. Close your eyes, and attempt to "see" yourself exactly, as you're reading this book.

Is your back straight or bent? head cocked, tilted, or upright? legs or ankles crossed? clothing smooth or mussed?

Then move a hand. Is the movement fluid or bumpy? Can you see it, in relation to the rest of your body, if you slow it down, or speed it up?

Cross (or uncross) your legs. If you're wearing trousers, how much ankle is showing, or if a skirt how much leg? Can you adjust this subtly?

These are exercises you can do for 30 seconds or 10 minutes, anywhere, any time of day, until you have consistently achieved the Outside Eye. And even then, for the rest of your life as an actor, add this exercise to your regular regimen of physical and vocal sharpening, and it'll give you an additional aspect of control of one of your major "instruments," as a theatre artist.

When the Scottish poet Robert Burns spoke of
*"...the pow'r the giftie gi'e us,*
*To see oursel's as others see us,"*
he was speaking of the **Outside Eye**, a mandatory "pow'r" for a disciplined actor!
*

"<u>Don't just do something – stand there</u>." (This was said by a director to a great, but mannered, actress.) He meant that Hey, it's OK to sit or stand <u>quietly</u>, watching and listening to the other characters without drawing attention by random movements. Just keep your inner life and actor's energy brightly alive, focusing on every word being said, so you won't fade away.

And when the focus is on You, "suit the action to the word, the word to the action," as Hamlet advised. Nothing arbitrary.

**Channel your energy by Shaking your Wrists, hard**.   This is
an excellent way to assure yourself of no unwanted movements.  If
tension builds up in any part of your body, it can manifest itself
unfortunately by trying to break free through jiggling hands or
percussive feet, or worse.

Whether it's Good tension in anticipation of the excitement
of performing your role for an audience, or Bad tension because
you're uncertain about that big speech with the foreign-language
poetry, or the always-iffy sword fight, you've got to Channel it,
consciously.


Before the show, and before each of your entrances, simply
**Shake Your Wrists with all your strength** (Not your arms, just your
Hands – at the wrists.  Shake them like crazy).


This primitive exercise provides two very important benefits:


It Reduces all the Tension throughout your body, sending it
sailing out through your fingertips.

and:

It Generates Actor's Energy, delivering you onto the stage
full of vigor and in control.

\*


**Always keep your weight distributed equally onto both feet.**
If you lump most of your weight over just one foot, you'll look like a
cartoon character, or as if you're about to launch into a middle-
European folk dance. Equal Balance is what you seek.


Standing with the toes of one foot a few inches up in the air,
with the heel planted on the floor beneath them, is a cute position
for a silly character trying to capture an elusive thought – for about
three seconds.  After that, it becomes a contrived pose.  The
audience doesn't want to see the sole of your foot.  Plant it solidly
back down onto the ground.

And:  **When you complete a Cross, be sure to stop with
equal weight on both feet,** as suggested in Chapter 7.  Sometimes
your Cross will be stopped in mid-step by another character's line,
or entrance, and you're caught with the toes of your rear foot digging

into the ground, with the heel raised as if you're waiting for the starting pistol to begin the 440 sprint. When this happens, just slide that wayward foot immediately into a graceful landing, dividing the weight of your body equally with the other foot, in a normal stage stance with both feet always flat on the floor in a T formation.

*

### Every Emotion must affect and inhabit your ENTIRE body

– including your feet. It would be ludicrous to see you, angrily roaring your heart out, clenching your fists, thrusting your arms at your victim, all the while your feet are turned inward, pigeon-toed, like someone at a first middle-school dance.

Or sitting, crushed by horrible news just received, with your legs crossed, relaxed.

If you've arrived on stage in full control of your body, you'll let each emotion in its turn penetrate into every cranny, manifesting itself to the audience from your left earlobe all the way down to your right big toe. And your Outside Eye will watch, and correct, and approve.

*

There aren't many characters who may be permitted to shuffle their feet: one might be an aged farmer whose crops have been totally destroyed. Otherwise: No. Not you.

**Pick up your feet**. In some theatres, many of the audience's eyes are at the level of the stage floor, so your feet will hold their attention throughout the performance. Your patrons will be dumbfounded to see the dowager empress or the captain of industry scuffing along like that aged farmer with the rotting soybeans.

Also, the ground cloths covering many stages can never be made totally clean, no matter how diligently swept and mopped , so shambling feet will dislodge many previous shows' legacy of grit, accompanying your movements with an unwanted granular percussion sounding like wire brushes, or a soft-shoe sand dance, but without appropriate musical accompaniment. Unpleasant grating sound effects aren't of any use to any performance.

When walking on the stage, lift your foot, and Lead with your Toes, reaching out to grab the next piece of floor, or earth, and then move assuredly to overtake those toes; then reach out with the other foot, carrying yourself with certainty and presence step-by-step across the stage.

*

Standing with your feet parallel and very close together (in what is called a Narrow Base) weakens your stage presence, because it makes you look as if you could be toppled by a gentle breeze. Unless you're playing a feeble, weak-willed character, this is an ill-chosen appearance, and you can prevent it by **widening your base, placing your feet 12"-15" apart**, which give you the strength to be deserving of the audience's notice.

**However, even with the wide base, if your feet are parallel, like railroad tracks, you'll look like a cardboard cut-out,** and when you speak, or start to move from that position, you're going to look pretty silly, and very clumsy.

It's better to always keep your Upstage foot Forward, and in fact to actually place your feet in the modified T-shape, as described in Chapter 7, which also allows you to focus on other actors on the stage, speaking in the direction that either foot is pointing, without having to change position.

*

Always when standing, **plant your feet, clutch the floor by digging in with your toes,** and **tighten your buttocks.** Yeah, I know that sounds hilarious, but try all three of these techniques at the same time, and you'll see how it straightens you up and makes you a commanding figure whom the audience is compelled to watch.

It also strengthens your voice production, which is a nice side-effect. You'll draw power from the earth, and send your lines powerfully to the rear of the House.

This position also prevents your rocking back and forth on your feet, another unwanted manifestation of uncertainty.

*

**Keep your feet flat on the floor even when you're sitting**.
The Outside Eye must ring an alarm bell when you slip into
comfortable but sloppy positions.  Resting your foot on its side, or
letting one foot creep on top of the other, are onstage images to be
avoided - unless they're deliberately-chosen mannerisms.

**Crossing your legs** is a good alternative, IF the period of the
play, and your character traits, allow it.  In doing so, keep your legs
relaxed, and gently point your toe so you won't flash the audience
with the sole of your shoe, because where that shoe has been, and
what it has stepped on, we'd rather the audience not be faced with.
So even if the foot is in the air, attached to a crossed leg, keep the
sole Flat, parallel to the floor.

*

If your character has been hurt, always **Favor the injured
area** in succeeding scenes, until the arrival of medical help and/or
the passage of time in the plot would have eased the pain.
Especially on film and tv, where scenes are shot out of sequence, we
see too often a character with a twisted ankle walking with no
hindrance just a few minutes later.

Hew closely to the time frame, and let a damaged arm or
jaw, or burned finger, be sensitive for the proper period, subtly
manifesting its tenderness without Indicating.

*

# Your hands are NOT as big as footballs. It just seems that way.

**"What can I do with my hands?"** This is one of the earliest and most fearful questions asked by new actors.

"There they are, embarrassing me, those long hinged arms, ending with huge meaty hands, further encumbered with five multi-jointed banana fingers each, and each with a mind of its own! And they're always visible to the audience! Even when the rest of my body is fully hidden by clothing, and even when there are Gloves covering the hands, they're still completely on display!!"

Do not fret, please! **Those two hands and ten fingers are some of your greatest friends, and most useful tools.**
When there are logical props available (a cup, pencil, hairbrush, newspaper, etc.) those hands are put to good use in maneuvering the objects to further delineate your character, to specify the time period of the play, to advance the plot, to get a laugh; or just to solidify the realistic nature of the production, as you wash dishes, concoct a cocktail, shine your shoes, sharpen a knife, or tie a policeman to a chair.

And there's no such thing as being solo on stage, even if there are no props nearby, because those hands and fingers, themselves, are right there with you, always – personal props to be used when needed or wanted.
Thank Mother Nature for being the ultimate Prop Crew, giving you fingers to snap, or to count, or to interweave, or to tie your shoes (or take them off), to scratch your bottom, to examine the seams of your shirt for fleas, to pry the wax out of your ears, etcetc. And your hands can clap, beat your chest like a gorilla, or push all the dishes off the table.     Boy, are you a lucky actor!

*

When you're standing, there's nothing wrong with simply **letting your hands rest normally** as Nature intended **straight down alongside your legs.**

Be sure your palms are facing <u>in toward</u> your legs.  Because if the palms face straight Upstage, your knuckles are presented dead on to the audience, making you look like a Neanderthal; or if your palms face straight Downstage, you look like a forlorn victim of a pickpocket.  Keep it simple, and let your <u>Thumbs</u> alone face the audience.

And that's where the hands should remain, parallel to your legs, slightly (oh, say 15%) cupped - <u>until there's a reason to move them</u> - either an External reason, such as shaking hands or picking up a flag - or - an Internal reason, when anger causes you involuntarily to clench them into fists, or your need to explain brings them up and forward to illustrate your thoughts, or fear causes you to touch your mouth and your chin, or cover your ears.

In every case, use your hand(s) cleanly and economically – no uncontrolled waving about, nor "sawing the air" as Hamlet cautioned, yet as many politicians still do, ineffectively trying to make a point.

Then, when there's no longer a reason for their being on display, <u>tuck them neatly back alongside your legs</u>, palms partially cupped alongside your thighs, in readiness to spring back into action when called for.

And be sure that those arms are <u>Relaxed</u>, because, unless it's a specific character bit, **standing with your arms tensed, or pressed Too Tightly to your sides makes you look nervous** (or just plain Scared).  If you've thoroughly shaken your wrists offstage, this should be easy to avoid.

*

<u>Jamming your hands into your pockets</u> can graphically illustrate a moment of frustration, or, contrariwise, determination. But get them back into sight fairly quickly.

Likewise, to show a casual moment**, <u>sliding your hands into your pockets might be a good character bit</u>**. But ONLY in that informal situation, and only briefly. Otherwise, it's evident that you're trying to sequester your hands out of sight.

And keep them flat while in the pockets; if you make them into fists it'll look as if you're smuggling baked potatoes.

Briefly stated:  USE those small and supple, un-football-sized hands, or simply let them hang naturally, in repose at the end of your arms. Out in the open. It's safe out there, it really is.

*

<u>Clasping your hands together at arm's length, down in front of you, is a weak and self-protective move, and should be avoided</u>.

And if you clasp your hands tightly together **Behind your Back, your arms disappear**. Try it in front of a mirror. You look like a big carrot. Hold onto that image.

*

"Little Hans" was a case study by Sigmund Freud, and "Little Hands" is the habit of some actors to **gesture <u>Only with their hands, ineffectively, flopping at the end of dead arms, which remain obdurately stationary at your sides</u>**. Hey – if the point your character is making is worth lifting one or both of your <u>hands</u> for, it's worth bringing the <u>arms</u> out into play, too.

**<u>And that means your Entire arms</u>**. One of the funniest/ saddest sights on stage is the ludicrous maneuver called "water wings," when an actor Yes, lifts up his arms – but lazily only the <u>Lower</u> Arms, pinning his elbows to his sides and flapping Half of his arms. Water Wings. Grotesque!

<u>**Air The Pits**</u>. This is a command often given to dancers, and it's equally valid for actors.  The "pits" are the armpits, and "airing" them means opening them up to fresh air by moving your arms out and away from your body, into the air, when External or Internal stimuli move them into action.   It's strong and effective. (And <u>theatrical</u>, which is ok!)    **Air Those Pits!!!**

<u>**And in a situation when you choose to gesture with One hand only, let it be your Upstage hand and arm,**</u> or you'll cover your body (and the 'Magic Triangle') and ultimately upstage yourself.

Try it, try using only your <u>Downstage hand</u> for the movement you seek; you'll realize how weak, and clumsy, and covered, you look.

*

Actors in <u>silent movies</u> carried over many of the "conventions" of 19th-century melodramatic theatre into their films, which are still available for us to watch for examples of **<u>Bad Use of the Hands,</u>** such as:

- <u>Clasping fingers in supplication</u>: *"Please stay with me, Prince Romanov!"*
- <u>A fist to one's own forehead</u>: *"Oh, why did I abandon my child?!"*
- The palms of <u>both hands placed over the heart,</u> and then opened up to your partner: *" Your sweet love will always be with me."*

You'll never be given such melodramatic dialog, unless you're in an historic revival (which actually can be very rewarding), but even in a contemporary production you can slip into physical clichés as outmoded as these 100-year-old examples.

It should be noted that it was Konstantin Sergeyevich Stanislavski (1863-1938) who almost single-handedly brought the theatre of the western world out of those external styles of acting and into an emphasis on characterization and honest internalized emotion.  His "System" was brought to the U.S. in the 1930s and rechristened "The Method," which is the basis for most approaches to acting today.

Whether you consider your emotional style to be The Method or The System, or something more modern, keep that Outside Eye always looking for, and correcting, 19th-century clichés, whose dispositions are literally in your hands.

*

**Keep your hands away from your mouth**.
You need a clear passage for your voice to travel to the back of the House, and covering your mouth will impede the straight line through the audience that you need for vocal projection.  It'll also hide your expressive face from those folks in the back row, who not only want to hear every word but see every emotion which generates and is generated by those words.

*

When stage business calls for you to slap someone, I say **Go Ahead and SLAP him**. But for safety, please hold your fingers, including the thumb, tightly together as a unit, and as Flat as you can make them. A loose thumb could break a nose or put out an eye – not a smart move if you want to retain friendships within the company and keep the stage floor free of blood.

Aim carefully for that area on the recipient's cheek that was made by a benevolent Nature purely and exactly to fit your conjoined fingers:  the big fleshy triangle between the cheekbone and the jawbone. Place yourself at the exact distance from that cheek so your arm will be out fully straight when your hand connects with it – and then give it a try, slowly and softly to begin with.

Work out the blocking with your director so you're able to **use your dominant arm for the slap;** right arm, if you're right-handed, and, uh, well, the other, if you're other-handed. This gives you the absolute control that you need for an effective, noisy (and safe) slap.

Obviously you're not going to smash the poor guy with a desire to hurt him, but you aren't going to give him a little whiffle patty-whack, either. **Use the same strength you would with a badminton racket** (NOT a tennis racket)**,** and, after you've rehearsed it a couple of times, and learned the correct distance and the correct force, you'll be rewarded with a superb *c-r-a-c-k* that'll bring the audience forward in their seats.

**Then Follow Through** with that swinging arm until your hand comes all the way around and hits your opposite shoulder, as you utter a small but audible exhalation, a Yip, expressing the energy your character has invested in that slap. This looks and sounds very real out front.

**If you're the Slap-ee,** I must advise you that, Sure, it's going to STING a little, but not much, and Hey, that'll get you deeper into the mood of the scene, Yes?
The second you feel the open palm touch your face, **snap your head**, in the direction that the slap would be propelling it, and let yourself **voice a definite Yip, an "involuntary" sound of person-being-hit,** a quick but heartfelt 'ohh,' or 'uh', or whimper, which adds to the realism of the moment.

Be Very, Very Careful **not to anticipate the blow,** by flinching or wincing or closing your eyes, nor moving your face in <u>any</u> direction until flesh connects with flesh. Otherwise you're liable to put yourself out of the safely-rehearsed path of the slap, and directly into harm's way, ending up with a damaged nose, or eye, or ear-drum, and that can spoil your timing. And it looks terrible to the audience.

**Other schools of thought on Slapping** (from people who fear that an actor's mis-timed hand might inflict permanent damage) believe that **flesh should Never touch flesh,** except **two hidden and smartly-clapped hands** at the supposed moment of impact, at the same instant that the Slap-ee issues a vocal sound of pain (a Yip, as above) and snapping back his head as the Slapper's hand comes abreast of his cheek – but misses by a millimeter, fooling the audience into thinking they've seen an absolute beauty of a smack.

This <u>Sound of Two Hands Clapping</u> is necessary, and may be created by the **<u>Slap-ee himself, smacking his hands together,</u>** at waist level or below, but only when they're fully covered from the audience's view by the Slapper's stepping in to administer the slap.

Or, if that positioning isn't possible, then **<u>someone</u>** in the crowd (There's going to BE a crowd, Yes?) <u>**directly behind the slapping duo, can time a hand-clap along with the supposed apparent face-slap.**</u>

Rehearse the hidden Clap until it sounds just like a Slap, and not a Pavlovian invitation to start applause by the spectators.

If the action of the scene intensifies to the point <u>where</u> **<u>Hands become Fists, and Slaps grow into Punches,</u>** then **Flesh should absolutely NOT touch Flesh,** and you really want to insist on **<u>a trained Fight Director</u>** to safely choreograph the adversarial characters.

*

Enough talk about fists and slaps. Let's get romantic.  **<u>When you hug someone</u>** as a gesture of Love, <u>clasp your dear one's back,</u> or shoulders, or neck, and **<u>Not your own other hand,</u>** narcissistically at the nape of your partner's neck.  You love your lover, not yourself.

*

# Chapter 10

# Use Your Props; not the other way around.

**A fine way to illustrate your character is how you handle props** – lighting a cigarette (well, maybe not so much today), shining your shoes, pouring tea, peeling potatoes, texting a message, counting coins, and the like.

And more: Your emotion can also be clearly presented to the audience by how you handle props - a gun, a fork, an apple, an envelope – and of course the props carried on your body, as combing your hair, working a toothpick around in your mouth, hiking up your shirtsleeves, taking off your glasses . . and even better, as discussed in Chapter 7, by STOPPING a piece of business with props as you receive the stimulus to begin a Transition.

Some examples could be: Starting to drink, but stopping with the glass halfway to your mouth; reading a letter, but stopping and slowly lowering the page; unbuttoning a shirt, but slowly letting go and standing back.

All is, and always should be, in character, using the prop as your character would, which strengthens the three dimensions of the person you're playing.

*

If you're not familiar with a particular prop or costume piece, and how to handle it, **be sure to get hold of the real prop early,** or a Very similar rehearsal prop, and use it and use it and use it, until it's second nature, so instead of being a time-bomb in your hands it'll be very comfortable to deal with in performance.

Such potential onstage adversaries that you must work with right away might include: needle and thread, monocle, can opener, Scotch tape, drinking from a military canteen, finishing off the contents of a glass, walking with a cane, folding dust covers by the end of a specific line, dealing cards in cadence with the dialogue around the table, loading a gun, and more of the same.

*

**<u>Props are inanimate objects, without minds; to let them Use
You is tantamount to surrendering your humanity to them</u>.**  Never!!

I once saw an actor play a lion in a children's play, in a
superb costume that was effective, comfortable, and charming, and,
best of all, had a glorious Tail.  That tail had been cleverly designed
and built to move with the actor, emphasizing her words and her
emotions, and marking her clearly as King of the Beasts, and
monarch of the stage.

But this actor didn't trust the tail, so always carried it,
holding onto its tip, restricting it from standing tall and majestic, and,
truthfully, making her look like a scared pussy cat.  No matter how
much the director implored, and ordered, the Lion within a few
lines of entering the stage would grab for the tail, and never let it go.

A sad waste of a tail.

And an illustration of how a prop can control an actor.

But not <u>you</u>, Right?

\*


**<u>When using a telephone,</u>** whether an old land-based
instrument or a tiny pocket phone**, <u>hold the mouthpiece opposite
your Chin,</u>** rather than cover your mouth with it <u>or</u> with your hand,
muffling your words and hiding your face.


\*

**<u>Monologues need props</u>** – both in an audition and within a
play.  Maybe only a wedding ring, bracelet, eyeglasses, a necklace or
lavaliere, a handkerchief, or a book. It's appropriate to give yourself
something to do with your hands, as well as to help express your
character, both externally and deep inside.


\*

**<u>If you partially hide a prop,</u>** with your hands or your body**,
<u>the audience will focus on wondering What Is That</u>**? **-** which isn't
where you want their attention – so keep everything out in the open.

BUT:  You're <u>not</u> in a tv commercial, holding the prop out,
stiffly, saying: "My new deodorant keeps me pleasurably dry."  Just
use your prop naturally and, as everything you do on stage, make it

easy for everyone to see and understand, unless the playwright is deliberately teasing the audience, hiding evidence.

*

**If you place a prop on a table, too close to the edge, the audience will thereafter be focusing on it, fearful that it'll fall.** Thus may an inanimate object wrongly steal focus from its human handlers, so please set the prop toward the <u>center</u> of the table.

*

**If you're blocked by the director to refill a glass, be sure you've emptied it first.** Pouring more liquid into a glass while there's still liquid in it looks foolish.

*

**Be careful of live flames** – candles, matches, and the like. Even if <u>You know</u> all precautions have been taken, audiences may worry, so make it clear that everything is safe by not allowing the flame anywhere near curtains or your clothing, or anything flammable.

In some states and cities, it's against the law to have a flame on stage. That settles That problem.

*

**It can be very effective to use a prop as a stand-in for another person.**

If that person is on stage with you, you can angrily hit the table as a substitute for his face, or embrace the back of a chair as a stand-in for her, passionately.

To call up the <u>memory of an absent person</u>, you can look at the door where she exited, or the sofa where we have seen him sit, or an urn of cremated ashes, a piece of jewelry or a man's pipe, or embrace a piece of the absent person's clothing.

\*

**If anything goes wrong on stage** (and sooner or later it surely will) **correct it, quickly.**

**If a prop falls** when it's not supposed to, **pick it up** smoothly and set it right as soon as you can – in Character, in the Style of the production, and in the Emotion that you're then playing, without breaking the rhythm of your dialogue. You know that the audience sees it (as they see Everything) and will be staring at that prop until you give that moment closure; then you and they can forget about the fallen prop and get your attention back to the play.

But, if the errant prop can't be whisked back into place easily, then, **if the style of the production allows it, deal with it entertainingly.** In Theatre jargon: Use It.

In a performance of "The Madwoman of Chaillot," one of the Countess's several underslips – with a stiffening ring all around its lower hem – came loose from its moorings and fell to the floor. The actress, in character, said: "Ooooh, my goodness," and stepped up and out and away from the garment. And there it sat, round and white and stealing focus . . . until the actor playing The Ragpicker came to the rescue. He said, "Pardon me, Countess," and picked up the slip, turned it on edge, and rolled it like a large hoop, all around the stage and then sailed it off into the wings. The audience loved it, as they always enjoy being privy to "backstage secrets."

Approach other onstage problems the same positive way.

If the phone doesn't ring on cue, you should say, "Hey, there's the phone," and answer it, continuing the dialogue as rehearsed. The audience will probably be well aware that they didn't hear a phone ring, but they have no time to dwell on it, for you've driven the play professionally well beyond that clumsy moment, and everyone's happy.

If a small prop (a key, a coin) is missing, keep your hand closed, as if you're holding the object just the way it was rehearsed all along. The audience wants to believe everything you're doing, and you're helping them do just that.

If a bottle or jar won't open, simply put it aside and forget it, and continue in full control, without making a big deal of it.

But if the error just can't be hidden or sidestepped, **turn the misstep into something positive,** as the actor did with the Madwoman's slip and, if a laugh wouldn't hurt the performance at that point, then go for it, and get your laugh.

In a hot summer performance of "A Thurber Carnival," the actor playing Ulysses Grant in the comedy sketch, "If Grant Had Been Drinking at Appomattox," also had roles in four other scenes, and the quick change into Grant was achieved with more speed than accuracy. His hasty dresser and his perspiring face prevented his trademark black beard from sticking firmly to his chin.

As the action proceeded, the beard became looser and looser, and each time it started to slip the actor gamely patted it back into place, without losing his lines or his character. But when it became obvious that the scene still had a long way to go, and the blasted beard wouldn't behave, the actor said to the other soldiers on stage, "Well, I think I'll shave!" and he deftly whipped it off, and plopped it onto his desk. The audience, who had been growing more and more uncomfortable as they watched the beard losing traction, roared and applauded, and then settled down to enjoy the rest of the scene, with a beardless U.S. Grant.

When it will best save the moment, and not interfere with a dramatic scene, **Draw a circle around it,** as those inventive actors did. But: If such comic solutions would be injurious to the moment, then you should just efficiently and with no nonsense carry (for instance) a fallen garment to the wings and drop it out of sight; and in the case of a slippery beard, just turn upstage and quietly pull it off and hide it on the desk. Yes, Sure, the audience would see these moves, but if you've handled them quietly and quickly, and professionally, the play can continue, with the glitches forgotten.

In Edward Albee's "A Delicate Balance," on Broadway, the actor Hume Cronyn was making drinks, but the two dozen or more ice cubes in the ice bucket had all become hopelessly stuck together in one huge amorphous mass. While speaking some of Albee's finest dialogue, Mr. Cronyn tried clunking the frozen mass against the bucket, and then tried prying a few cubes loose with his fingers, all without success.

The audience was beginning to titter at his dilemma, so he eliminated the distraction by holding the large cluster over a standard-sized drinking glass, and said wryly, "I'm afraid this isn't going to fit," and returned it to the bucket, at which the audience, relieved of their concern, gave him a hearty, thankful, and forgiving roar of laughter, applauded his resourcefulness, and everyone got back to the business at hand.  This was in the early part of the play, before the real drama had begun, so the laugh was in keeping.

In a heavily dramatic scene, or a full-fledged tragedy, the way to handle such a situation is Not to handle it.   In this case, just make the drinks with <u>no</u> ice, and leave the ridiculous-looking clump in the bucket, out of sight.

Be very careful, in the face of these unanticipated glitches, that you not make things worse.  When you pick up a fallen prop, get a firm hold of it, so you won't drop it again, compounding the situation.  And when you improvise (ad lib) a line that saves the day, <u>say it strongly and positively</u>, with the same projection and energy that you've been using all evening with the scripted dialogue.

If, as often happens, the actor seems to be <u>apologizing</u> for an ad lib, with breathless vocal fear, or in a tiny, barely-audible squeak, the audience will reflect that discomfort, and the next few minutes will be unbearable for you and for them. No, No.  Charge ahead, with actor's energy and stageworthiness, and leave the error behind.

However:  **<u>Beware the actors who deliberately CAUSE PROBLEMS, just so THEY CAN THEN SOLVE THEM, humorously or heroically</u>**.

This happens even in long-running, professional shows.  A bored actor deliberately spills a drink, or drops the muffins onto the floor, or dances his partner into a chair, causing her to fall.  After which he covers the 'accident' with a funny line he has previously prepared, and seems to all to be a clever fellow.

This is selfish, self-aggrandizing nonsense, and can't be allowed. Everyone in the cast and crew must be dedicated to giving the audience the Best Performance Possible, exactly as rehearsed – and - if problems develop unexpectedly, to solve them appropriately, and move on; but never to be the intentional Cause of the interruption.

*

**When Eating onstage, Take Small Bites**. Ask the Prop Crew to cut your food into bite-size pieces, or do it yourself, so you never have to speak unintelligibly with your mouth full of a big chunk of food, nor take the chance of choking, by swallowing a big bite quickly, so you can get to your next line.

**The same is true for Drinking**, from a glass or a cup **– Just take small sips,** so you won't drown or spill, when it's suddenly time for your line.

*

This wouldn't seem to be a necessary warning, but, sadly, it is. **Real liquor should be forbidden onstage**. The wisest theatres have an overall policy of No Alcohol or Drugs in the building, ever. Or in anyone's bloodstream beginning four hours before the performance.

But I've twice seen performances where uncontrolled lack-of-art resulted from alcohol. Give the audience a buzz, not yourself.

In one performance of a play with a lot of drinking in it, the director thought it would be "fun" to put real liquor in the onstage bottles. After the three leading actors had been drinking the real stuff all through the play, one of them, sitting on the sofa, sozzled and uncomprehending, heard the other two, who had realized that she was out of it, carrying the plot forward by re-working her lines to fit their characters – as she fuzzily tried to understand how those somewhat familiar words were sailing by over her head.

In one of my own productions, one of the actors checked in very late, and was rushed into the dressing room by a suddenly-relieved stage manager, who didn't realize that the actor was late because it was his payday, and he had stopped off for "a drink" with his friends.  In the first few minutes he was onstage, nothing seemed wrong, but pretty quickly the stage lights warmed up his innards, and it became evident he was quite drunk.  He began losing control, garbling words, and in a bit in which he was supposed to stop another actor from running around the stage, he robustly body-checked him, knocking the poor guy painfully across the floor.

As soon as he exited, I ran backstage to confront him, but found that I wasn't needed.  Some of the other cast members had shoved him into the basement shower stall, with torrents of cold water splashing on his head, and non-stop coffee from the vending machine poured down his gullet.  Any words from me would have been superfluous.

As would any more be here.

*

# Chapter 11

# EYES ARE THE WINDOWS OF THE SOUL

*This image has been used by many writers, including Tennessee Williams in his "Camino Real," so I feel comfortable in appropriating it here.*

Always let us see your eyes – for Yes, they <u>are</u> the windows of your character's soul. Even when the character is downcast, keep your eyes up, letting us see them projecting despair.

Keep your chin resting on an invisible shelf, so the high angled stage lights illuminate your eyes, through which we see what's going on Inside.

As you duck your head, or hide your eyes, or hood them, narrowing them into impenetrable slits, or drooping the eyelids shut, you're cheating yourself of a major tool, and your audience of its main access into your character's core.

\*

EYE CONTACT between actors helps strengthen every moment. It makes total sense that you should look directly into the eyes of each person you're speaking with on stage. It reinforces the reality for you, and for your partners, and definitely for the audience. Then why is it that so many actors look over the shoulders, or at the foreheads, of their onstage colleagues? Or look at an invisible barrier six inches in front of their own eyes? It's because they're uneasy, unsure, unrehearsed, unable to join in the very necessary ensemble cooperation that makes a performance work. And it's very destructive to the play.

I once had an actor tell me: "No, I can't look him directly in the eyes; he's too intense." Ah, but that's Why you should give him eye contact – sharing that intensity drives the performance strongly along its rehearsed track, as you reinforce each other's concentration and camaraderie.

If your attention is wandering, or you're just going through the motions, and a serious actor looks into your empty eyes, all you'll be presenting is the back wall of your cranium. (That's not a physiological fact, but it's a theatrical reality.) You'll have deprived your colleague of the mutual cooperation that bands a cast together, and gives the audience true confidence that this is a well-rehearsed ensemble troupe to whom it's a pleasure to give their attention and their belief.

However: Beware:  <u>Eye Contact must be accompanied by your always-present need to have your face and voice available to the audience</u>.  If you lock <u>both</u> your eyeballs in contact with <u>both</u> your partner's eyeballs, then Someone is going to get Upstaged. Perhaps both of you will.  So: Here's where you both must **<u>Cheat</u>!!**

"**<u>Cheating</u>**" is a perfectly acceptable bit of stage technique, which **allows you to maintain Eye Contact, but continue to remain Open to the House**.

If you **each look into the other's <u>UPSTAGE</u> eye,** <u>with Your Upstage Eye</u>, and each of your bodies is in that cherished ¾ **position,** it will give you both the stability of Eye Contact, and still keep both of your faces (and "magic triangles") open to the House.

Your director may often holler (gently, we hope) from out in the House: "Jeannie!  Cheat!!"  This means simply keeping your Upstage eye looking at the action on stage, but opening your face more toward the audience.

You'll also hear the call to "Cheat!" when production photos are taken of the play.  Do it, or history will be full of pictures of the back of your head.

*

"**<u>Counting the House</u>,**" the old-fashioned term for staring straight out into the audience, **is generally forbidden**.  It looks as if you've broken the Fourth Wall as well as the believability of the world you've created among yourselves on stage.

It's permissible, of course, for a Narrator and for an actor delivering an aside, to play directly to the House. Additionally, a director may choose **one special moment in the play, for you to look straight out front,** as if opening your heart to the world. But avoid making eye contact with anyone out in the audience; in fact, the wisest course is to look out over everyone's head.

In the days of the actor-manager, the star could often be seen literally tabulating the size of the audience, to be sure he received his contracted percentage of the ticket sales; thus the derisory label, "Counting the House."

\*

**When you're looking out a window, or through scenic shrubbery toward the wings – SEE something.** All that you'll really see may be some of the furniture standing ready for Act II, or the stagehands watching a muted football game on a small tv, but by tapping into your own storehouse of images you will convince the audience that there's a wounded soldier or a carnival barker out there. If you can't do that, if you can't bring an affecting image into the forefront of your mind, then the audience will see through your eyes exactly what you see – backstage ordinariness. They deserve better than that.

It's another exercise you can work on at home, anytime. Create something real in your line of sight, when there's nothing there, and then bring these images to rehearsal, just as you bring your voice and body, always ready.

\*

Filmmakers can use a close-up lens, to focus the cinema audience's attention where they want it. In the Theatre, Lighting Designers can shine a follow-spot, or angle an instrument onto the stage to specifically isolate an actor or a group. But you always have something with you, simpler and more immediate: **Your eyes, sharply focused, can tell the audience exactly where to look.**

The director will have chosen the focal point she wants the audience to see - let's say two men standing at the bar - and she'll have given those actors business that will draw the audience's focus. But it's a large stage and someone out front may glance over at you, sitting quietly at a table. However, instead of reveling in this attention and drinking noisily from your glass, stealing focus, you should already have been looking directly at the bar scene, so your eyes will divert any glances from you immediately to the guys over there, where the director intended. It's an instantaneous eyeball-deflecting shot: An audience member looks at you, but in a split second his focus is tossed across the stage. Better – and more subtle - than a follow spot. And a true mark of an ensemble player.

*

**To avoid another character's eyes**, as part of your stage business, you first have to <u>let the audience see that you've made eye contact</u>, and only then can you break it. You have to Set it up (engaging each other's eyes) before you can Knock it down (disengage). The audience has to see it happening, or else it hasn't happened, and an important moment has been lost.

*

Chapter 12

# The Actor's Voice

This book doesn't pretend to offer Voice and Diction lessons, for there are many fine texts and teachers in that specific field. No, this chapter just presents some practical vocal hints to add to your storehouse of Technique, and to carry into rehearsal with you.

**Lips – Tongue – Teeth**: These are the tools in and around your mouth with which to form the words the playwright gave you, which you're going to project out into the audience. If you're not using all three of them, but manufacturing the spoken words somewhere in the middle of your mouth or the back of your throat, they'll be malnourished, indecipherable and fall uselessly into the orchestra pit. A sad ending to a Shylock soliloquy, e.g.

So: **Keep your voice in the FRONT of your mouth**.

Even (or Especially) when you're playing an old curmudgeon, or a dying person, you can't give way to the cliché of talking through imaginary cobwebs, "blub, blub, blub." Sure, wobble the vowels a little but, as with every character you play, articulate your words with those lips, tongue and teeth, and be sure that, however feeble or eccentric a person you're playing, you make every syllable clear.

We in the audience have GOT to understand all that you say, always. Or you needn't bother saying it.

*

To be heard by every member of the audience, **Focus your voice,** throwing it **like a tennis ball** toward the rear of the House, all the way to the last row and, if there's a balcony, then to the last row of the balcony.

During a break in your first rehearsal in the actual performance space, go into the auditorium and reconnoiter the back wall, to find a visible target for your voice. An Exit Sign, a decorative panel, a space atop a door which allows a little sliver of light to come through - - any specific tangible end point that you can see clearly from the stage, toward which you can consciously send your voice with every word of your dialogue, on a direct, straight line.

The audience, between you and that target, will benefit as your voice travels strongly amongst them.

*

As stated elsewhere in this book – and it bears repeating - **"Volume" does not mean "Yelling."** An audience does not like to be Yelled at, and anyway a yelled line most often springs from a tight throat, so it becomes tortured mush by the time it reaches the audience's ears. And has irritated your throat, paving the way for laryngitis!

Whether you're in a simple conversation or portraying an angry moment, your lines should not only be presented with full Volume, and also with complete Clarity.

To achieve this:  **Support your voice, Keep your throat Open, and Reduce Tension in all parts of your Body**.

Before every entrance in every performance:

**Yawn deeply and thoroughly** (which clears the passageway of your throat) and **at the same time, Shake both your hands** (as discussed in Chapter 8) with all your might (<u>Not</u> your <u>arms</u>, just your hands – at the wrists). These exercises reduce tension throughout your body, giving you absolute control of all parts of yourself, including an uncluttered airway through which your clear and supported voice may flow.

*

Be especially careful to **Support each line of dialogue all the way to the END**, avoiding the lazy American habits of swallowing the last syllable or making every sentence swing upward like a question. ("Like, I was talking with Barbara yesterday?") (NO!)

Drive all the way to the <u>Period</u> before you breathe, and only then release the support. (British call the Period a <u>Full Stop</u>. YES!)

*

**Maintain the Pace of your voice, always within your control**.
Yes, your Actor's Energy must always help you stay vibrant on stage, always Leading the audience - but be careful not to <u>outrun</u> them, speaking so fast that nobody can understand you. You'll exhaust everyone, just trying to keep up with you.

By the same token, **you can't allow the audience to Get Ahead of You**, to anticipate where you're taking them, or they'll just tune you out, from sheer boredom.

How do you keep them with you? Simple: **Tight cues!**

I'll say it again: **Tight Cues!!** They keep the audience right alongside you, hanging onto your words and enjoying the journey. Tight cues also move the play along, buckety-buckety, making it a whirlwind experience, but one that's well-modulated for the cast and audience alike.
And they're simple to accomplish:

First of all, you've got to **Learn Your Cue lines,** which throughout the play are <u>the last five or six words of another actor's line leading into your line</u>. Some actors just wait until everyone else has stopped talking, and then realize it's their turn to speak. Yikes!!!
Now – preparing to say your next line, you're armed with the other actor's Cue Line, so: instead of waiting for him to Finish saying his <u>entire</u> Cue line, you must **SPEAK INTO** the Last Syllable of that line. **OVERLAP** his Final syllable with your First syllable. So you're both talking at Exactly the Same Time, for the length of **that one single syllable**. Strongly, unapologetically, with full volume.

"Oh, No! Won't the audience then miss a lot of the dialogue??!!!"
Not at all. Their ears will sort it out. It's just like ordinary human speech, with our daily conversations overlapping all the time. What can be maddeningly <u>U</u>nnatural on stage is the awful pause that occurs between every spoken line, if each actor waits till each cue line has been completed, and THEN speaks. It sounds like

computers are speaking – One Line, Pause, then Another Line, then Another Pause, then Another Line . . . . . . Pfui!

I've seen as much as ten minutes cut from the running time of a play, just by encouraging the cast to Tighten their Cues.  And of course it's not just the chronological time that's saved – it's also the psychological time.  As the play moves along tightly, the action is sprightlier, thus the audience is more conscious that Something Important and Interesting is Taking Place Here – and they move their bottoms to the edges of their seats.

*

A terrible, and too-frequent imposition these days is the **hanging of microphones on actors' clothing, or above their heads, or languid in the footlight area.** Serious and well-trained actors should **resist this practice**, and prove it's unnecessary by filling the auditorium with their natural, well-projected, well-supported and non-amplified voices!  It also helps the audience identify from whom each voice is emanating.

*

**Develop and nurture your Outside Ear** (similar to the "Outside Eye" discussed in Chapter 8) to always hear yourself as the audience hears you.  Check for, and correct, any problems in Breath Control, Volume, Dialect, Tight Cues, and Proper Emphasis.

This is one more bit of homework you should assign yourself, even when you're not currently rehearsing.  Just sit comfortably and read something silently - dialogue from a play, a page of a book, a newspaper article – and rehearse in your mind how you'd like to speak those words on a stage.

Then read them aloud.  LISTEN to yourself.  Are you speaking them the exact way you have prepared those words, those sentences, in your head, with pauses and stresses and builds?

If not, why not?  Work on it until you know you've reproduced the passage as you'd planned.  Then find a second passage, and work on it.

It's another valuable tool for the serious actor. For you shouldn't wait for the director to tell you what you sound like in rehearsal, and call for more Volume or Clarity.  You should be your own best judge, by exercising that Outside Ear, whenever you're rehearsing or performing.  Never turn it off.

*

The best playwright gives the actor many wonderful tools to work with: poetic imagery, strong character traits, stirring soliloquies, suspenseful scene endings, and many more.  But <u>some of the greatest gifts from writer to actor are</u> <u>**Balances**</u> and <u>**Three-Builds**</u>.

<u>**The Balance**</u> is an almost algebraic equation giving two opposite sides of an argument, or an idea, which forces vocal variety onto your speech pattern, pulls the audience irrevocably in to the dialogue (thus the plot), and gives them a clearer picture of this character.

Here are a few Balances:

"Neither a <u>borrower</u> nor a <u>lender</u> be"

"<u>To be</u> or <u>not</u> to be"

"..since I cannot prove <u>a lover</u>..I am determined to prove <u>a villain</u>."

Seek these gifts of the playwright throughout your script, these two-sided swords for you to play with, and rehearse how best to present them.

The point is to contrast the first word or phrase with its antithesis, its opposite.  You can "weigh" the differences with your hands, as if with a scale; or with your eyes, looking in one direction and then the other.  But the Balance is best illustrated with your voice.

State the first part flatly, simply declaring the word clearly - - and then <u>contrast</u> it with its opposition word, changing the emphasis of your voice to indicate that something new and different is coming .. and thus achieve your Balance.  Try it with those examples, above, and find some of your own, in literature and in daily speech.

<u>**The Three-Build**</u> is another grand and useful implement in your tool-kit, and when the playwright (as all the good ones do)

hands you a three-build, cherish it and brandish it.  Here're a few examples:

"I hate you – I loathe you – I despise you!"

"I looked for his body in the bedroom – the kitchen – and the basement!"

"And be it moon, or sun, or what you please..."

"Away, you scullion!  you rampallian!  you fustilarian!

"Is the chair empty?  Is the sword unswayed?  Is the king dead?"

Your job now is to implement this vocal build – by increasing volume and/or intensity, word by word, from the first to the third, demonstrating the importance of this thought or this feeling.  You're showing the audience that it's not just This Vital, but it's THIS VITAL, and, even more, it's T H I S   V I T A L!

And of course you can reverse this procedure, and **take the Three-Build DOWNWARD**, which also shows great importance.

Start High: "I  L O V E   Y O U"
then more gently: "I ADORE YOU"
and then very softly, both vocally and emotionally:
"You're everything to me."

LOOK for three-builds in every script, be delighted when you find them, and then thank the playwright, by doing as you're asked, in building those words or phrases Up or Down.

*

**Assiduously check Pronunciations** of proper names in your script (people, places, etc) and also of Any word which may be unfamiliar to you, and find its definition.  Then: Even though you've done all this research, remember that the audience has Not.

So:  You've got to <u>speak more clearly than usual any word that they're liable not to know,</u> or they'll miss important plot bits.

No, of course I'm not suggesting that you spoon-feed them ("Heeeere's what I'm sayyyyyinggggggg!  Do you understannnnnd?" Pfui!  No!) - but do be very careful; support your voice, pronounce each unusual word or phrase exactly, and perhaps <u>throw in a tiny Pause before saying the word</u>, to let the audience know subconsciously that this is a moment worth extra attention, as you're reminding yourself that it's due special articulation.

Otherwise, there'll be a dozen little whispers through the seats:  "What did he SAY??!!"  And that's no fun.

\*

In the rare events when you are blocked to speak directly upstage, you must consciously **project your voice back over your head and behind you,** straight to that spot you have selected in the rear of the auditorium as your vocal target.  With your mind's eye, SEE that location, and THROW your words – Not into the upstage wall of your set, but the Other Way, way back, back, back to the farthest corner of the House.

In arena or thrust stages, this is a must on <u>every line</u>, for some of the audience is <u>always</u> behind you.

\*

<u>Avoid stressing Personal Pronouns</u>, **except** to strike a Balance - "I hate HER, but not YOU".

That's ok.   But how unrealistic does this sound?:

"We decided to stop at Brian's house, to see HIM, and take HIS mother to the movies."

or:   "Katie's nice. SHE's a schoolteacher."   NO!!

### <u>ALSO</u>: <u>Avoid stressing Adjectives</u>.

Well, for goodness' sake, then, **what CAN an actor stress**?  Ah, my friend, **NOUNS and VERBS**, nouns and verbs, just as you do in your daily colloquial speech.

Give yourself the assignment of listening to your friends talking casually, and hear Yourself, too, every day - - and confirm the fact that the words mostly emphasized in normal speech are Nouns and Verbs.

The audience is unconsciously aware of this fact, too, so will feel the <u>wrongness of emphasizing</u>, for instance, <u>any of these</u>:

*"We were going to THE store, pushing my LITTLE brother in the BROKEN stroller."*

(Try it this way, aloud; and then again, NOT stressing the adjectives, and see how natural it feels.)

\*

**Never pronounce the Article "a" as a long "A",** as in "c<u>a</u>ke," but always "UH," as in "<u>a</u>ttempt."

Try it:  Say these sentences aloud, <u>breaking this rule</u> and pronouncing the "a"s as in "cake":

*"Give me <u>a</u> little hint, <u>a</u> clue to <u>a</u> better life."*

*"You're <u>a</u> prince, <u>a</u> gentleman and <u>a</u> scholar."*

And then say them again, as in normal speech, sounding the "a"s as in "<u>a</u>ttempt."

When you hear an actor, a teacher, minister, politician, etc, hit those Long "a"s, you can be sure they're <u>reading</u> the speech, or reciting a memorized piece - - but None of the words have come from the brain or the heart, or even spent a few minutes there.

\*

Find the opportunity to **<u>Play Against an expected emphasis</u>.** Actors who declare "There's only way to say 'I Love You'" (for instance) are full of baloney!  You can easily imagine saying those

Three Little Words in different-from-expected emotions. Try "I love you" wrapped in each of these moods:

Anger          Hatred          Fear

Disgust        Revelation      And, what the heck: True Love!!!

This is true of any lines in any play. The unexpected can help you to solidify a unique and specific character.

*

Avoid "grocery lists." When a playwright provides you with a speech containing a Series of words or phrases, it gives you a wonderful opportunity to display your vocal versatility, by giving its own special meaning to each item, as if you're just that second thinking of it – and then when you think of the next, and then the next, share these thoughts, these images, with us at the moment each seemingly occurs to your character, but never as a grocery list.

In Shakespeare's "Richard II," the king tells of his fears:

> For God's sake let us sit upon the ground
> And tell sad stories of the death of kings:
> How some have been deposed, some slain in war,
> Some haunted by the ghosts they have deposed,
> Some poisoned by their wives, some sleeping killed,
> All murdered.

That passage contains a SIX-Build, which gives you too big a handful to pile one "death" directly upon the other, as in a THREE-Build - - but you've got to be sure you're not mouthing the dreaded "grocery list," either.

It's easy, as suggested above. Just let each new fear come to you afresh, and color it with the intensity with which it affects you - - sometimes, Yes, building Up, and then Down; one phrase Louder, one Softer; an image of Agony, then Horror, perhaps --- but ALWAYS steering clear of burbling out a List.

Here's another exercise: Try giving each phrase its own level of importance in this speech by Duke Senior in Shakespeare's "As You Like It," as he describes his happiness at moving into the Forest of Arden:

> *And this our life, exempt from public haunt,*
> *Finds tongues in trees, books in the running brooks,*
> *Sermons in stones, and good in every thing.*
> *I would not change it.*

Read these passages aloud, deciding on a specific import to your character of each separate image.  When you're successful at that, no series of phrases will ever seem to you as a "grocery list."

*

If you start to deliver a monologue as if it IS a monologue, your audience will shut down, or sneak into the lobby and never come back!  "Whoa! Here comes a Big Speech!  Bye-Bye!!!!"

So: **Begin a monologue as if it's just a Single Sentence**.
Then, let the first thought engender a Second thought in your mind, which you then give voice to – and then another, and another, until, by golly, it's a Monologue, and the audience never realized it!

That's a fine example of one of the chief principles of good theatre:  **The Illusion of the First Time**.

You know that, if you grab a big lungful of breath, and stand extra tall, showing that you're getting ready for a l-o-n-g speech, the chances are that no one will want to climb that emotional or oratorical mountain with you.

If, however, you begin with the single sentence:
*"Oh, what a rogue and peasant slave am I!"*
- as if you're simply berating yourself with one little insult, the audience will be right there with you, wondering how you'll react to being your own attacker.

And then a new image comes into your mind, a comparison with one of the traveling actors, to show how MUCH of a rogue you consider yourself to be:

*"Is it not monstrous that this player here,*
*But in a fiction, a dream of passion,*
*Could force his soul. . . ."*

As you pile each new complaint upon yourself, each comparison of yourself with the player - as you think of each new self-accusation seemingly ON THE SPOT - you're letting the audience see Hamlet's thought processes, which helps them know more about him - - - and you're Not speechifying a long, hard-to-follow gaggle of words, which holds your listeners at arm's length.

\*

It's in your power, and in the power of your voice, to **Top almost any noise, rehearsed or unrehearsed**, that reaches the audience's ears. You learned in rehearsal about door slams within the action of your play, and underscoring music, offstage sound effects, etc, so raising the volume of your voice, riding over the top of them is already part of your pattern.

But in performance you must become aware immediately of noises beyond your control and then, by increasing your volume appropriately, <u>pull the audience's focus back to you and the play</u>. Sirens and honking horns can penetrate even the most soundproof theatre, and each venue has its own problems. I once worked in a summer theatre right next to a suburban train station with frequent arrivals, and outdoor theatres endure the nuisance of traffic sounds, shouts, barking dogs, crying babies, etc. You can top them all, if part of your mind remains conscious of such intruders.

However, there's one horrendous noise that even the most barrel-chested, stentorian actor **can't drown out: Airplanes flying over an outdoor venue, or a theatre in a tent**.

I produced a summer theatre which offered both of these performance spaces – Children's Theatre in an open-air amphitheatre, and the Main Stage in a tent - and we learned right away that we couldn't out-reverberate airplanes, especially slow-moving "flying boxcars," so we decided to accept them as part of the environment, with this ploy:

The instant that the onstage actors heard approaching motors on high, they'd stop talking, and all very slowly turn their faces toward the direction of the plane, and follow its progress with their eyes and a slow movement of their heads as it came closer, and then passed overhead, and then continued on its way. As the sound diminished sufficiently for the actors to be heard, they'd bring their heads back to their normal positions, and <u>go back one line in the script</u> from where they'd stopped, and start to speak it a little louder than normal, and reduce the volume as the plane noise totally disappeared - - exactly as they'd do in holding for a laugh (See Chapter 14), or holding for applause, with the addition of a wise and tolerant gaze at the plane's trajectory.

And indeed there always was laughter as soon as the audience realized that the cast was following the path of the plane with their eyes, and applause as the plane went its way. They often applauded even earlier, as a tacit "Thank You."

Of course, when we were playing a drama, we didn't seek a laugh, so the actors merely stopped talking and remained in their positions, not moving, until the plane had passed.

Audiences not only accept such stoppages of speaking, but they welcome them, so they don't miss any of the dialogue, and don't watch an actor trying to dominate an all-encompassing sound.

*

### <u>Avoid speaking in an abnormally high pitch (falsetto)</u>.
When imitating someone else (e.g., a screechy woman or child, or someone with an unusual speech pattern), usually for comedic purposes, many actors sharpen their voices to such a stridency, such a high pitch, and constrict their throats so tightly, that they create a screech that is totally unintelligible – and pretty unpleasant, too. And watch out, because this straining can damage your throat, at least for the current performance, and maybe permanently.

Remember that **the higher the pitch you aim for, the more support and enunciation you need**.

All in all, it's best to avoid the tense voice and just imitate the Tone of the person you're parodying, while keeping your throat open and your articulation sharp, with major vocal support.

**There is one time when you Want stridency, and that's during Vocal Warm-Ups**, when you <u>Increase tension to Release tension</u>.

Here's just one simple exercise in this regard:

<u>Tighten your jaw and your throat</u> and scrape out the word *"niiiiiiinety-niiiiiiine"* and then relax and say the word again, with smooth beauty: *"ninety-nine"*.

Oh, Yes, at first make yourself sound like the Wicked Witch of the West being squeezed by elevator doors, screechy and knotted up beyond belief. And then immediately <u>un</u>-clench everything, and say it again with an open throat, producing a clear, mellifluous tone that would make a concert singer jealous.

This release-of-tension, coupled with a Big Yawn before every entrance, will help toward the smooth clear passage of your voice.

*

If your character must speak in <u>a Dialect</u> – either foreign or regional American – **avail yourself of the marvelous audio tapes, C.D.s, and downloads** on the market today – or, even better, <u>try to find a person</u> who comes from that locale, and speaks with that dialect, natively, and who will agree to work with you, correcting your errors, until you have a good handle on the proper speech pattern. Your director can help you find such a model.

*

**You should be proud of** the heritage – your parents, your home town - that has helped create **your own personal speech**

**pattern,** its rhythm and dialect, and it would be a shame if you let anyone talk you into abandoning it. It's a great part of who you are.

But if you plan to spend much time on the stage, and are assembling all the "tools of the trade," you should work also to **attain what's called Standard Speech,** a generic, non-regional, American voice pattern which can be learned from the texts and tapes mentioned above.

If available, there's nothing like learning Standard Speech from <u>an experienced (and on-the-spot) teacher</u>, who can point out areas where you're improving and where you need more focus.

Then, when you're offstage in "real life," you can continue to speak with the voice you know to be You, that you've never allowed to be lost, but then easily assume Standard Speech when you go to auditions, or start rehearsals.

*

We carry a proud pioneer heritage in our language and the varied dialects that have derived from the hundreds of origins of our forebears mixed with American regionalisms. But:
<u>We have All apparently long ago tragically decided to eliminate the word "and" from our vocabularies, and replace it with the single letter "n"</u> – as in "Rock 'n' Roll," "Guns 'n' Roses," "Nice 'n' Easy."

This is fine for a company name, or a band, but it's infiltrated our daily speech as well, and **it must be kept off the stage,** unless you're playing a very casual teenager.

To hear this sad elision clearly, say this sentence aloud, and listen to yourself:

"Winnie and I are going to New York to see some shows; maybe 'Guys and Dolls,' or 'The King and I,' and then drive home with Corky and Michael."

How many "d"s could you <u>Not</u> hear, especially in those treacherous areas where the word following "and" <u>begins</u> with a "d", which tends to blend those two "d"s together, usually eliminating one or both of them.

The word "and" appears many times in every script, and needs constant attention.    Sound those "d"s!!!

*

The FIRST THREE LINES <u>you utter in any play are Vital to your relationship with the audience</u>!

If your voice is weak and your manner apologetic, they'll write you off as unimportant to their notice, and it'll be an uphill climb for you the rest of the evening, trying to win back their trust.

But if you arrive on stage, saying (silently, within your mind, and In Character) "Here I come to save the day!!" you'll have their attention for the whole play.    On your first entrance, as always, employ **Actor's Energy, and Full Vocal Support**.

*

Speaking of THREE LINES (and in the Theatre as everywhere else in life, the number THREE is a constant touchstone): <u>When you have more than three sentences in a single speech</u> – **Always Impose Vocal Variety!** Or the audience will be lulled by your monotony.

Lines by a good playwright will probably by themselves force you into making an emotional transition within any contiguous three lines, or at least raising or lowering your tone, or speeding up or slowing down your voice and your movement.

But these are things well within your control so, even if the author hasn't provided you with the clues, you must find the stimulus to vary each three-sentence grouping, because after any speech of that length, <u>unvaried</u>, the audience has tuned you out.

*

When you are directed to **Speak some Lines from Offstage,** you want to be sure the audience can hear and understand them, of course, for they're necessary to the plot, or to your character - or they'd have been cut from the script.

Check out the scenery on the side of the stage you're to speak from, and **find the most porous part of the set,** where your voice has the best chance of getting through to the onstage actors, and thus (more importantly) to the audience.  Maybe a window, or an open door, or a gap between flats, where you can stand (out of sight of every area of the audience, certainly) and then project and focus and support your voice as you TOSS it, like that vocal tennis ball, over several hurdles and through several blockades, toward the spot at the back of the theatre you've chosen as your vocal target.

If you're in the midst of a costume change, as often accompanies lines from "the other room," or picking up some props to bring on stage, be sure you've worked it out with the Crew to have everything you need close to the set, so you can do your offstage business efficiently, while still being able to speak through the scenery, and be heard out front.

*

When you whisper (*Sotto voce*), or "throw away" a line, **it's still got to be heard by the audience** – very clearly, and with your voice strongly supported and focused toward the back of the House.

**The same is true of Ad Libs**, which must never be introduced for self-aggrandizement or showing off, but only to cover, gracefully and maybe even humorously, an error on or backstage.

If ever you find that you <u>have</u> to Ad Lib, make it loud and clear, and **Believe It**.

*

In the moments before the first performance of the beautiful play for voices, "Under Milk Wood," there was a lot of logistical and emotional turmoil, for its playwright, Dylan Thomas, had left in a taxi the new closing pages of the play, which he'd rewritten that day.  So he frantically jotted down the new lines, as well as he could remember them, and handed them to his fellow cast members, as they all ran to the stage to take their places on their stools and place their scripts with the scribbled new pages onto the music stands in front of them.

As they could see, below the front curtain, the house lights dimming, Thomas loudly whispered to his frenzied colleagues: **"LOVE THE WORDS."**

Oh, Yes. Whether your backstage pre-show moments are smooth and quiet, or disjointed and upsetting, remember - in every role you play - Dylan Thomas' simple request: "Love the words."

*

**When the script calls for you to say the same word or phrase twice in a row, Make them Different.** The second time they're said, the words should be either stronger or weaker; or louder or softer, as determined by your emotion.  Otherwise the character wouldn't be repeating them.  Try these, making the repeated words different:

"Quite so.  Quite so."

"You're lying to me!!  You're lying!"

"Who's there?  Who's there?"

"You're terrific!  You're terrific!"

*

**When speaking, put the Question mark on the Interrogatory Word, the word that Creates the question**, not at the end of sentence, which you do when you're writing.

If you ask: "Why did you walk away?" you want the word "Why" to contain your question. If you flip the word "away" up into the air with a questioning tone, it's unreal, it's distracting, and it's sometimes unintentionally funny.

Try to place the Question Mark on the Question Word:

Where did you find it?

How can I learn to drive?

When do we eat?

*

**You've got to make a vocal sound when you fall**, or trip, or hit someone, or someone hits you, as part of the action of the play (as illustrated in Chapter 9). I call it a "Yip," but it's <u>any</u> "involuntary" expostulation – "uhh" or "yee" or "jeez" or "ooouu" or any sound that would bounce naturally out of your startled character's mouth.

If you're silent when you've been bumped or slapped, the audience will think it's an accident, or, just the opposite, <u>they won't believe it</u> in the context of the scene.

It needn't be (Mustn't be) big and showy – but just as large as the "injury" calls for, and <u>at the exact Instant</u> of the "hurt". Too early or too late and the audience will laugh At you, and that's something we never want.

*

**The pronunciation of the words "either" and "neither" can be a tricky one**, and that's one of the many decisions you're faced with in selecting your character's traits.

It may seem unnecessary to mention this, but many actors who, in their everyday speech, say "EYE-ther" and "NYE-ther," are reluctant to switch to "EE-ther" and "NEE-ther," no matter what their characters' backgrounds are. And some don't even think about it, accepting "EYE-ther" as common to all English-speaking people. It's not.

*

# Chapter 13

# Create Artistic Reality

<u>Every style has its own reality</u>. Even in a Farce, or a Fantasy, you mustn't abandon the truth of your character or your emotions. Remember that the **audience depends on the actors to give them a sense of Reality,** of Belief in what they're doing, which gives each spectator something to hang on to, to be just as involved in the production as the cast is.

In fact, <u>the farther from reality your production goes, the more Real you must play it.</u> Nothing is worse in a children's play, or a musical comedy, or an expressionistic play about amoebae on a stylized stage set representing Eternity, than actors playing "at" their roles, patently acknowledging that "this is all make-believe, so why should I try to convince you otherwise?" Nay, Nay! BRING the audience <u>into</u> your unreal world by the <u>artistic Reality of your work</u>. Be specific in your choices, your moves, your handling of props.

The language, the scenery and costumes, music, dance – these aspects of the production will carry the less-than-real style, while You must have bedrock belief in who your character is, in all that you're doing and saying. The actor carries the reality.

*

<u>Whose house are you in, when you enter the set</u>? Or whose office, porch, ship's cabin, cherry orchard, etc?

The whole ambiance will be different, depending on whether it's Yours or someone else's. And who that someone else is. You'll relate to the furniture, the props, the view out the window, in totally different ways.

As you create the reality of the <u>location</u>, you're demonstrating another way of illustrating your character traits.

*

You must be <u>conscious of all aspects and conditions of each</u> <u>moment of the play,</u> such as the Weather, the Temperature, the Season, the Time of day, etc.  Not all of these stimuli will be useful or needed in every scene, but if you know that the character has been awake for 20 hours, or that it's overly hot – or cold – in this setting, or the dead silence leading to a storm has enveloped the house, you must carry the awareness of that condition, for it could affect the mood of the scene, and of your character.

It's not necessary to wave your acting in the audience's face, Indicating as you pantomime the unspoken lines:  "Brrrr, I'm shaking with chilblains." or "Ohhh, I've never been so tired."

But remember how You react to extremes of temperature, to late hours, to crashing thunderstorms, and bring those memories to the stage, via your character's traits.

Stifle a small yawn, subtly pull a small area of your shirt away from your "perspiring" skin, unobtrusively cup one hand over the other, to "warm it up," or listen for sounds of approaching rain or something amiss upstairs.

If You believe it, We'll believe it.

*

<u>When your character is looking for something on stage, be</u> <u>sure to really LOOK for it, at a place where it might be found</u>. Something the size of a boot won't be in a small drawer, or a diamond necklace inside the dishwasher.

<u>Picture it, in your mind</u> – What does it look like? What's its size? Where did you last see it?

And. Please, **take a while to find it**, because the members of the audience can't find anything they're looking for in the first place they try, so they know you couldn't either.

This, like so much of your Realistic acting, will provide the audience with **The Shock of Recognition,** which the playwright, the director, and You must always try to evince.

Remember that the audience sees Everything.

\*

Are you as tired as I am of tv heroines suddenly flipping their hair behind their ears, so the camera can see their faces, even when preparing to crouch over the body of a dead boyfriend, or aggressively accosting an enemy, or submitting to a passionate kiss??

As if one's appearance takes precedence over the ordeals of this moment.  No.  Never!  **Your responsibility**, knowing what's ahead of you on stage, **is to arrange your hair** (or your wig) during costume fittings, and certainly in your dressing room <u>before</u> each performance, **so when you get on stage you know your hair isn't hiding you from the audience**, and your thoughts and emotions are focused on the subject at hand.

**The same is true of a hat,** whose brim can easily shadow or hide your face from a large part of the audience, so fasten your cap or hat onto the back of your head, so it's attractive and a good character statement, but allows full visibility – and then Forget It!

\*

Even if a prop you've been given is much lighter than the object is supposed to be, as often happens with, e.g., suitcases and boxes, **you must convince the audience that it's suitably heavy**.

According to theatre lore, Marlon Brando, in his early days as an actor, used to partially fill a drinking glass with water and mark its level by a streak of nail polish on the outside.  He'd carry this glass around with him, constantly hefting it in his hand, to impress its reality on his "kinetic memory," I guess you'd call it; and then he'd pour out the water and carry the empty glass around, recreating the feel of its weight when the water was there.  He'd do this, it's reported, with successively different amounts of water.

OK, that's perhaps a little extreme, and may have been his joke in the face of all the stories about his Method training -- but the Idea is a good one.  I've seen several productions of "Death of a Salesman," in which it was evident that the sample cases Willy carries on at his first entrance were light as feathers, and not weighed down by his wares, as well as his unsuccessful career.

Away and apart from rehearsal, find objects of the approximate weight of things you must lift in the play, and record in your memory how they affect your hands and arms, and your legs and your back.  No nail polish needed, but you can tell any nay-sayers that you're carrying on the Brando tradition.

*

### Playing drunk on stage means playing NOT drunk.

In life, a person under the influence doesn't <u>try</u> to stumble, or to drop things, or slur words – but does <u>try to walk straight</u>, to handle objects deftly, to speak clearly, to sit carefully on a chair - - <u>but doesn't succeed</u>, and that's the point.  It's these unsuccessful attempts that are your ways of portraying intoxication.  Trying to force uncooperative legs or hands or tongue to move smoothly is one more task you must soberly set for yourself.

*

**When you read something aloud on stage** – a letter, or a label, for instance, **the audience must really believe you're seeing the words for the first time.**   In fact, this is more easily done if the words are Really there, on the prop piece of paper. Ask your director if this is possible.

But be careful not to get too accustomed to those "new" words on the paper, but see and read them fully afresh, each time.

*

Here's a good realistic piece of business that you might try (once in a performance):  **When you're leaving a table, get a few feet away, and then remember that there's something left behind that you need**: a pen, a letter, a what-have-you, and go <u>back</u> for it. This happens to your audience, every day of their lives.  And they'll love you for being as human as they.  Another Shock of Recognition.

*

## If another character says: "Stop Yelling!" – you'd better have yelled!!

I think that explains itself.

Similarly: "I can't hear you," and "Please sit down," and "Don't walk away from me!"  It's all there in the script.  Trust the script, and act accordingly – ahead of the other guy's line.

Likewise: When given a request or an order by another character ("Come Here," "Get down from there," "Please sit," etc.) **wait for the Full Line to be said before doing as you're asked.**

Too, if another character's line is "Stop!" and it's slow in coming, then please keep going.  Exit the stage, exit the theatre, exit the town, until you get the proper cue to halt.

Haven't we all seen plays (or tv shows) where the heroine shrieks "Get your hands off me!" before she's been touched?  Or someone sits a split second before hearing the line, "Won't you sit down?"  Sure, these would make fine moments in some comedies, but not in O'Neill.

And: When asking a question, give your partner ample time to (not) answer, before asking it again. ("What's the matter?-I said-What's the matter?" with no pause in between is the mark of staginess, not of truth.)

Then: When you repeat the question, of course, vary the intensity or pace significantly from the first time.

*

Every person in the audience has at one time eaten spicy food, and drunk hot coffee, and some of them have drunk liquor – so they know that many kinds of food and drink will bring about **an involuntary reaction of their lips or tongue or taste buds,** and **you'd better give them that reaction.**

Not big or overblown (Not Indicating, in other words!) but the folks watching you from out front have to experience that Shock of Recognition, even with food and drink.

*

**If emotionally difficult lines flow from your lips too easily, the audience won't believe you,** because they know that THEY have trouble saying things like "I think I love you," or "It was me that did it." (Or, too rarely: "It was *I* who did it"!!)

Only a desensitized oaf would blurt out "Your husband's dead," without having trouble forming the words; or "The doctor says Mom has cancer."

Feel the closing of your throat as your larynx tries very hard to speak through the emotion.

If the audience realizes that these words are coming to your mouth too readily, they're not going to give them any credibility.

*

You may have performed the show many times, but tonight is this audience's first view of it, and **they deserve to share the Illusion of the First Time,** every moment. Each line, each transition, each movement must be presented by you as freshly as indeed it was on opening night. KEEP your performance new and avoid the staleness and obvious repetitiveness that even moderately long runs can inflict on unaware actors.

To accomplish this, **Seek new Images** when the tried-and-true stimuli begin to fade; find new approaches to filling the pattern that the director and the other actors – and you at your best - expect.

*

If the script calls for you to be in pain, make it **Specific Pain.** A toothache is different from a broken ankle, and not only because it's in a different part of the body. Each has its own level of intensity, of duration and frequency. If you've never actually experienced the required pain, speak with a doctor or nurse, or someone who's been there.

*

**Play the moment.** The old theatre adage is: "Hamlet can't anticipate the end of the play during his first scene." Yes, he's going to die, and so is Richard III, and Romeo, and Willy Loman, and the Thane of Glamis (See Theatre Superstitions, in Chapter 18), and even

Mister Roberts . . . . . but the characters can't project that ending during earlier scenes, and in fact the more Life you bring on stage, the more startling will be your death when the playwright springs it on us.

And this specific admonition – Play the Moment – applies to Each Moment of your performance. Shut out every other thought, about the play or anything else, and focus on This Moment, on what your character is feeling, saying and doing. And then the Next Moment. Each clear and specific.

*

Even the finest playwright sometimes gives you lines full of complex philosophies, without even trying to make them sound like human speech. This then becomes Your job. Make the lines your own!! Take them away from the lecture platform, and set them in the everyday locale of the play. Phrase them as if you're thinking of them just a split second before you say them, and you'll conceal the fact that you've been tossing the author's heavy-handed opinions around the stage.

Modern French plays, particularly, tend to wave large polemics in the audience's faces. Calm them, break the slogans down into bite-sized mouthfuls, turn them into sincere beliefs of the character, and you're likely even to convert the audience.

*

### Make Decisions. Make Choices. And let the audience see you making them.

**Decisions and Choices** are often tightly bound to **Transitions,** which, as we've seen (in Chapter 5), are guideposts the audience needs to proceed through the play, up the Lightning Bolt.

Without the character's visible **Decision** to kiss the man, or to steal the money, or to hide behind the door, or to use the phone, the audience won't become involved in the performance. If everything flows along with no recognizable Reason for your doing anything; if, in short, you're not sincerely involved, then the audience won't be either.

They want, and need, to share with you the **Moment of Stimulus,** so let them see it hit you, and then the ensuing **Transition** as you make the **Choice** to stay with the girl instead of flying to London, or to get out of this frightening house - NOT BECAUSE THE SCRIPT SAYS SO, but because your character weighs the pros and cons and CHOOSES to stay or go.  Very clearly show the audience the exact moment <u>when you make that choice</u>.

*

Although Aristotle (384-322 B.C.) in setting out the necessities of classical theatre only named Three "Unities": Time, Place, and Action, he would certainly have added **"<u>Unity of Style</u>,"** except that all the playwrights of his time were already conforming to one single (now classical) style, and didn't need to be reminded.

We, however, live in a theatre world of every conceivable style of writing, of acting, directing, and design, as well as the styles offered/demanded, by the many media.  Comedy-drama has been with us for a long time, and, on television has been rechristened "dramedy."  And the "Musical Comedy" of the early 20th century became "Musical Drama," beginning with "Show Boat," or, as some argue, later, with "Oklahoma!"

These well-structured amalgams break the rules by establishing New rules, which is the wonderful way of the theatre world – but Beware the director who, just for the egotistic fun of it, inserts farcical movement into the midst of a heavy drama, or in a comedy suddenly has the actors moving and speaking like robots – both of which, sadly, have actually occurred, as has even more breaking of Style.

No, you as an actor can't undermine your director by refusing to perform as you're asked, but you can, always, ask for a conversation before or after rehearsal, or on a day off, and communicate your discomfort.  After that, your only options are doing as you're directed or resigning from the show.

However:  <u>Unity of Style is in Your hands, too</u>.  You've got to keep an Outside Eye and Ear on yourself, starting at the first rehearsal, to assure that in the midst of the performance You are not drifting into a different style from the other actors, slowing down a farcical pace by dwelling too heavily on some possibly serious lines, or inserting uncalled-for slapstick business into a straight comedy.

*

**You must play IN the moment, not AT it.   In fact you must be "In In" it!** This is a useful, and deliberately repetitive expression coined by one of my acting teachers, the great bear of a man, David Itkin, who himself had been trained in Moscow's Habima Theatre.

It means, simply:  That if you Stay Outside the scene ("Phoning it in") you'll quickly tell the audience you're not fully involved, so why should They be?  Instead, focus your energies, your concentration, and all of yourself, to be not only <u>In</u> each moment, but fully "<u>In</u> <u>In</u>" it.

*

**Always play a Positive attitude,** for a Negative focus will make you invisible to the audience, or worse, an indecisive, insecure force on stage.

For example:  Let's say that your Inner Want (or Beat) (or Intent) (or other term that you work with, to frame and project your emotion) is Not to Touch Desdemona.  This Negative – backward – stimulus will cause your hands to tiptoe across your own chest, or fiddle with a goblet, or take your dagger out of its sheath, and then weakly return it, as you resist the need to Touch Her.

But:  Ho-Ho:  Re-phrase your challenge to yourself, so it's now Positive:  **You Want to Touch and Hold Tightly to Everything in the room EXCEPT Desdemona.**  So, Then you'll strongly grab the back of a chair while looking lustfully at the girl, and then move to that goblet and clutch it with both hands, wishing it were she, and then reluctantly put it down.  And the audience will see your dilemma, and identify with you, because you've illustrated your desire Positively – not weakly and uncertainly.

*

# Chapter 14

# Comedy

Even non-theatre people have, in recent years, thought to show their erudition by citing this famous – tho possibly apocryphal - death-bed remark:

### "Dying is easy; comedy is hard."

They variously attribute it to dozens of old actors, from Donald Wolfit to Peter O'Toole (who, still living, even quoted it in a movie), to Olivier and Gielgud.

But the actor most credited as the originator of this now clichéd line is Edmund Gwenn, the twinkly Englishman who, bearded, played Santa Claus in the original film, "Miracle on 34<sup>th</sup> Street."   BUT: the Gwenn proponents manifest their ignorance of theatre history, for, long before Gwenn ho-ho-ho'ed at Macy's Christmas tree, or in fact died, the "Comedy is hard" quotation had been laid at the bier of 17<sup>th</sup>/18<sup>th</sup>-century tragedian Edmund Kean – whose name unwitting quote-mongers transmogrified into 'Edmund Gwenn,' whom they had at least heard of.

Well, whoever said it, HE or SHE was RIGHT!  Comedy is terribly Hard, and not for the faint of heart, and certainly not for anyone to tackle lightly, unprepared.  For there's no sound so awful (in its true sense) than an audience's Silence as they stare unsmilingly at a stageful of inept actors playing a comedy clumsily.

A horse knows when its rider is unskilled, and resents having its time wasted.  So, absolutely, does an audience.
And neither unsuspecting audiences nor poor actors deserve to share that deathly silence.  So: Read On!!

\*

**Just as in the most weighty Drama, you must Believe every aspect of the character you're playing in a Comedy**, or the audience won't.

If you decide to "act Funny," rolling your eyes or punctuating your lines with inane sounds, or speaking directly at the audience while mugging, you'll deserve the ghastly silence coming from the House, and the sight of audience members heading for home.

As stated in Chapter 13:  The further your production is from straight Realism, the more YOU must be Real, and believe in your character.

Of COURSE you will always recognize the fact that you're playing Comedy – but Always from a solid base of Truth, and not of Foolishness.  ("But this lisp always makes my friends laugh!" is not a justification for buffoonery.)

*

And, along with absolute belief in what you're doing, **always bring into your comedy a Desire to Entertain!!**  Some people are better at telling jokes than others.  They approach you with an open face, smiling, their bodies full of energy, their voices light and inviting, wanting to give you a laugh.  You respond to such an invitation, even before you hear the punch line, smiling with the joke-teller and relaxing your body, trusting this guy to turn your smile into a wholehearted laugh.

This same Wanting to Entertain, Wanting to Engender a Laugh in the audience, Wanting to Imbue them with your same rollicking energy, must accompany you onto the stage every minute of a comedy.

A Heavy voice and Dour face will hurt a comedy performance exactly as they'd undermine a joke-teller at a party. Who wants to remain amid a cloudy atmosphere?

*

## When playing Comedy, keep your Eyebrows UP.

A clown's makeup is based on his painted eyebrows raised high over his eyes.  This reassures the kids that all is in fun, and he's not going to be hurt when the firecrackers go off, or if he's hit in the head by a giant sledge hammer.

So it is for us when playing Neil Simon or Aristophanes – If we keep our eyebrows UP, the audience will, too, knowing that, no matter how horribly contrived is the bad stuff happening to our hero and heroine, all will end well, and we can enjoy every pitfall along the way.

Meanwhile these open faces in the audience, created by their unknowingly raising their own eyebrows along with the actors, have prepared their muscles to easily and quickly open up a smile - and smiles give way easily and quickly to laughs – and that happy sequence is just what we're looking for.

Check it yourself, in a mirror.  Say this line (from "The Frogs," a comedy from about 405 B.C.) with your eyebrows in their usual, neutral position:

> *"Which is the quickest way to get to Hades?*
> *I want one not too warm, nor yet too cold."*

Not too funny, Yes?  But try it with your eyebrows raised – not uncomfortably so, but definitely higher than normal.  Even that tepid line is now worth a smile, and with ensuing lines and comic business, soon a laugh could develop, and an audience that laughs a lot enjoys itself, and those folks will tell their friends about your hilarious show, and they themselves will come back for the next one.

All because you lifted your eyebrows just a little.

\*

Here's the First Law, or the Holy Grail, of Comedy:

## <u>THERE ARE 3 PARTS TO A LAUGH LINE</u>, <u>which must be observed</u>:

- **The set-up**
- **The delivery** (often called the 'punch line')
- **The button**

To illustrate, here's a basic joke:

Jack: "The garbage men are here."
Ellen: "Tell them we don't want any."

Now: Applying our <u>3 Parts of a Laugh Line</u> to that joke:

**The set-up** is "The garbage men are here," a short piece of information the audience needs to know so they'll "get" the joke when it's delivered.

This line needs no particular emphasis or attention, as long as it's Clearly Spoken.

**The <u>delivery</u>** is the actual Joke, the Punch Line: "Tell them we don't want any." The person saying this line must not only enunciate it Totally Clearly with no pausing and no rushing of the words, but <u>Must Not Move</u> as she is saying it. Not her body, not her hands, not nodding her head – Nothing. <u>Not moving</u>.

OK, maybe that line is funny enough to need no help from the actor, but the audience in most cases has to be informed that that is the End of the Joke, and Ellen's not going to say anymore, so they can laugh if they like ("and the actors would prefer that they DO LAUGH, Thank You!!").

So this information, this instruction, this encouragement is conveyed by the **button.**

**The <u>button</u>** is the crisp, clean Ending to the Laugh Line, giving it Closure.

To achieve the first part of the structure of the Button, Ellen must **put a solid Period on the end of her sentence.** Not a comma, not a dot-dot-dot, not an upswing, not a downswing, but a pluperfect A-Number-One PERIOD.

**THEN:** Reinforcing that Period, Ellen will at the same milli-second do <u>**one clean, simple piece of business**</u>: e.g., setting her teacup into the saucer – clink!; or sitting herself down in one sharp movement – ploomph!; or zipping a zipper in one sharp movement – zing!; or shutting a door or a drawer, kerplop!; or turning her head toward or away from Jack, in one crisp turn – swish!  This brusque, clean, one-step movement, coupled with the Period, is your **button. The Laugh Line is complete.**

**Now:** <u>**Everyone onstage turns to Stone**</u>!  If Anyone moves an eyelid, the Laugh Line has been aborted, and you'll receive some watery ha-ha's from scattered parts of the House – but not the all-encompassing full-audience laugh you wanted, and worked for.

<u>To clarify</u>:
Jack says clearly: "The garbage men are here."
Ellen says clearly, without moving: "Tell them we don't want any." - with a palpable **Period** after "any," and at the <u>same moment</u> as the Period, she (for instance) closes her book – snap! - in one clean movement.

And then EVERYONE ON STAGE **TURNS TO STONE.** Not so-stiff-you're-vibrating, of course - but non-moving, non-talking, non-fiddling-with-props stone.

Q:  Why in the world are we all Turning to Stone??!!
A:  Because you're **HOLDING FOR A LAUGH**. You're indicating to the audience that it's ok, and desirable, for them to laugh right now, and you've stopped talking and moving around so they can guffaw, for as long as they like.

But:  If they DON'T laugh after the Button, and you've given them <u>one second</u> to do so, <u>you just immediately carry on with the next line</u>, Keeping your actor's energy at 100%, not letting the failure of the laugh line depress you, or slow you down.

<u>If they DO laugh, then Hurrah</u>!!  Continue to Hold for the Laugh, staying in your non-vibrating Stone persona - because they must be allowed to laugh <u>as long as they want to</u>, without fearing that

they'll miss some of the plot, or another good joke, if you start talking again while they're laughing.

So, please, <u>HOLD OFF on the talking</u>, because if you cut into a laugh, speaking too soon, then <u>The Audience WON'T Laugh Again</u> during this performance, because they now know that you're going to press on regardless, cheating them of their participation in the fun – their laughter - <u>and</u> of hearing the ensuing dialogue.

Then: Heaven help you, you're playing a comedy at which an audience subconsciously has decided to sit quietly and listen. Death!

Q.) All right, I'm Holding, I'm turned to stone. How long does the Hold last?

A.) OK, this is an area where Comedy really <u>is</u> Hard, because as the old aphorism has it, "Timing is Everything!"  But you can handle it.

In your Turned-to-Stone mode, and at your command, every follicle of hair on the back of your neck is at attention, sensing the length and depth of the laugh; the hammers and anvils and stirrups in both ears are vibrating with the sound of the laugh. And, attuned to that input, you're advising your vocal cords: Wait, Wait, Hold, Hold, Hold. . . . .

<u>Then, the split second that the laughter reaches its Loudest Point, and is just beginning to diminish, you say your next line</u>, but with More Volume than usual, since some of the laughter is still blocking some audience ears.

As the laughter continues to decrease, you <u>reduce your volume proportionately</u>, until the audience bottoms out to silence, and you're again speaking at your normal Stage Volume.  And on goes the play, with extra zip, for the audience is now part of the fun.

*

Q.) What if they laugh Unexpectedly sometime, <u>not</u> cued into it by a Button?

A.) Great!  **If they're finding funny moments on their own**, the playwright, the director and you have done a terrific job, creating a jovial atmosphere of free laughs.

This fortuitous new laugh could erupt because of a line that strikes the audience funnier than it did last night, or a prop or costume that won't behave, or someone in the house is laughing or reacting in a silly way, or an actor mistakenly bumps into another actor, or anything of the sort.  We may never know why.  But:

You do exactly the same thing as on <u>any</u> laughter from the House, exercising the Three Parts of Holding for a Laugh:

<u>The second that you hear **even one audience** member laugh</u>:

<u>YOU STOP TALKING</u>.
<u>YOU TURN TO STONE</u>; <u>you freeze in place</u>.  <u>Everyone</u> on stage does.
<u>YOU WAIT</u>. Hold, Hold, Hold. . . . .
As the laughter reaches its Loudest Point, say your next line with More Volume than usual, then bring it down to normal volume <u>as</u> the laughter fades, and you and the audience will carry each other to further peaks of comedic joy!  Or at least have a very good time together.

Q.) <u>Ah, but what if The Laugh comes in the MIDDLE of one of My Lines</u>??
A.) Almost everything in this technique <u>is the same</u> as Holding for <u>any</u> Unexpected Laugh.  There're just a few new twists:

**You <u>Stop Talking</u> Immediately**. (<u>That's a New Part.</u>)
Then, as usual:
You turn to stone.
You listen for the loudest peak of laughter, and Start Speaking again with greater volume. Except that (<u>This is another New Part.</u>)You <u>Go Back</u> and <u>Start Saying</u>, **from its Very Beginning,**The Sentence That was Interrupted by the laugh.
And, as with any Laugh, you then lower your volume at the same rate that the audience is completing their laughter. When the laugh is over, you're at normal volume.

I'm sure you can see Why you need to <u>re-begin</u> the sentence that was interrupted by the laugh. Let's say you had started saying:

> **"If he touches you . . ."**
> And then they laugh, out of nowhere.
> As the laugh ends, you finish the line:
> **"...I'll kill him!"**

Even if they only laughed for a few seconds, this murderous declaration, ("I'll kill him!") coming out of thin air, will startle and confuse them.  They need to hear, anew, the <u>entire</u> sentence.

> **"If he touches you, I'll kill him"**

Or:            **"What I really hate..."**
> Late laugh arrives, and lessens.
> Then you say:
> **"....is tapioca."**

And they don't know Why, out of a seemingly clear sky, you say: "is tapioca."

Believe me, every audience will appreciate your holding for the laugh, and then putting them back into the picture by restoring the entire interrupted line . . . . **"What I really hate is tapioca."**

And it's likely they won't consciously recognize that you've repeated yourself a little.

Haven't you been frustrated when the actors in a movie Can't re-start a line that's been drowned out by audience laughter? It's not going to happen, of course, and that line, as important as it may have been, is lost forever.

Theatre actors are much more accommodating.  Aren't you?

*

This exact same technique of Holding for Laughs is used when **Holding for <u>APPLAUSE</u>.**

Applause after a Song or a Dance is expected, and your choreographer or director probably ended your number with a Button, a Taaa-Daaa! as you came to a dead stop with your arms outstretched, or your perky head cocked as the music finished.

<u>Here, as with Laughs, you must Absolutely **TURN TO STONE**</u>.  If you move even a little, they'll think there's another verse, or you're going to start speaking, and they'll cut the applause off with a bread knife.

So you wait (stonelike!) for the highest peak of the clapping, and then come in with your next line, louder than normal, subsiding with the applause, and with the extra energy the audience response has given to you, and to the play, and to the clappers themselves.

But no one Exits (and no one Enters) and no one Speaks or Moves, <u>until the applause has started on the down side</u>.

Here's a nice twist you might have fun with:  If you've finished a love song, after which you're blocked to Kiss, **DELAY THE KISS.**  Hold For Applause, as always, and then **JUST BEFORE IT REACHES IT LOUDEST PEAK, <u>Then Kiss</u>.**

The applause will double and redouble in volume and enthusiasm, as the audience has been emotionally hit by the Kiss, and – unaware and involuntarily – poured their feelings into extra vigorous applause.

<u>But, apart from applause after a musical number, you can't pre-plan when they're going to clap</u>.  And if you expect it, they'll probably disappoint you.

Applause may (or may not) erupt when the curtain goes up to reveal particularly fine scenery; or on the entrance of a well-beloved actor; or after a nicely-delivered speech or well-timed comedy bit; or as an actor exits after playing a scene quite well.

<u>And then it's the old familiar Hold, the same as after Laughter or a Song</u>:

Keep your ears open.

Hear the clapping start.

Immediately turn to stone.  Freeze!

Note when the Applause reaches its loudest peak.

Start speaking again with greater volume (Repeating the beginning of the sentence, if it had been interrupted).

Ride the diminishing applause down, lowering your volume in proportion.

Arrive at your normal level of projection as the applause quietens to silence.

Be glad for it - and Hold for it, every time!  **An audience usually WANTS to Laugh, and WANTS to Applaud** - and, Oh Yeah, <u>You Want Them To</u>. Very much.  Allow them to express their enjoyment without interruption.

*

It should be noted that, in Miss Galflong's day, they taught that - in order to keep the illusion of "real life" - the actors should keep talking through laughs or applause.

But, so as not to waste the play's dialogue on unhearing ears, the recommendation was to repeat "Chicken Pot-Pie," over and over, so your mouth was seen to be moving.

If you've read about that technique in an old book, enjoy it as a bit of theatre history, **But Let It Remain in the Archives**!

*

**If one laugh is good, two are better, and three is heaven**!  If the "Hat Trick" of achieving three goals in a hockey game brings praise upon a championship team, so does winning three laughs on one line earn plaudits (at least among your fellow actors).

Building a triple laugh requires the same disciplines as described above: Putting a solid Period on the sentence, Holding for the Laugh and Turning to Stone. PLUS now some careful pre-planning.  It's not easy, and can often lead to nothing.  If you have a line that you feel contains within it Several possible opportunities to tickle the audience, here's what you do:

When you get your laugh on the first part of the line, you hold for it as usual - - but not for quite as long as you hold on a single-laugh line.  For you deliver the Second part exactly at the moment when the audience has reached the peak of its laugh.

You come in with full energy and a slightly increased volume, and the energetic belief that they're going to Love this next one.  And when they Do, and when their first laugh, which never ended, has billowed up and over and into a second laugh, you lie in wait for that one to reach its highest crescendo, and then with your full energy Top their double-barreled laughter with your Third, final, and best laugh line.

You've stayed in character throughout this whole process, you haven't changed your physical stance, and you haven't given a hint that you're going for a triple-play.  You've merely introduced a little extra vitality and volume, and have timed their reactions carefully - - and if you've done it all well (and the Theatre Gods are with you) you could literally have them rolling in the aisles.

The role of Dogberry, the foolish constable, in "Much Ado About Nothing," contains a lot of 16th and 17th-century humorous references which are largely lost on modern audiences.  But a few of his lines are solid laugh-getters even today, and there's one sequence that's a genuine blue-ribbon triple-laugh line.  Imagine an audience chuckling at the first line, laughing at the second, and roaring at the third - - as you top each successive bout of laughter:

> *Oh, that he were here to write me down an ass!*
> *But, Masters, remember that I am an ass.*
> *Though it not be written down, yet forget not that I*
>    *am an ass.*

Seek such playwright's treasures in each script you're given.

\*

Never forget, however, that some audiences will laugh very little, and some not at all, no matter how funny the lines, or how adept you are at building laughs.  This can happen on Tuesday and Wednesday evenings, or at a Benefit Performance for which they've laid out far more cash than a regular ticket goes for, or at any performance when the Box Office has not "dressed the house" correctly, leaving great gaps of "broken teeth" throughout the auditorium: two audience members next to three empty seats, then two more patrons, then five empty seats. It's hard for an audience to laugh when they're not clustered anonymously amid a large group. They feel nakedly exposed, with empty space all around them, and laugh timidly, if at all.

Such performances will occur, more often than we like, but **You Must Never Let An Audience's Silence,** <u>When You Expect Laughter,</u> **Discourage You**, <u>Nor Cause You to Change Pattern</u>.

What you must do is merely double-check to be extra sure that your face is open and your eyebrows up, that your energy and desire to entertain are at full throttle, that your belief in what you're doing and saying is 100%, and your cues are tight and your volume is projecting your lines throughout the audience.

If they're still not laughing, it's wrong to Hate Them. (I've seen that happen, and it drags the show even more into the depths.) And it's equally wrong to Push. Milking It for laughs (i.e. straining the smile on your face, or ramrodding the "Please Laugh" vigor and extra volume in your voice, as Flop Sweat runs down your spine) is a sure-fire disgrace, in the eyes of your theatre company, and in the thoughts of your audience, whom you'll alienate completely.

Remember that they aren't Required to laugh, but <u>We are required</u> to give them the best show we can, and not resent nor be troubled by their lack of response. I've seen performances when such seemingly-impassive audience members have come backstage after the show, full of compliments, remarking on scenes or lines they thought were hysterically funny. And I've bitten my tongue to keep from asking: "Then Why Didn't You Laugh?!"
It's their prerogative, and we must honor it. (!!)

\*

Throughout the entire performance of a Comedy (and throughout the comedic scenes in a drama) **Keep up the Pace**. I remember a director who prowled throughout the House during rehearsals of a comedy, chanting loudly and continuously,
**"P - A – C – E!    P – A – C – E!"**
Well, yes, that's too much – but the actors rehearsing or playing a comedy do need to have that mantra circulating constantly through their brainpans: **"P-A-C-E!!"**

**Attention to the detail of Pace is especially needed in Farce, the physical comedy** exemplified by the Three Stooges, "Noises Off," and in most productions of "The Comedy of Errors," and the Mechanicals' scenes in "A Midsummer Night's Dream," and many other great plays, both classical and contemporary.

A farcical bit (a man's toe is stepped on) grows to another (a tablecloth is tossed over his head, causing him to bump into furniture) and another (he steps into an open trapdoor and disappears) in rapid succession. If these bits are separated by too much time, or languid movements or speech, each may get a small laugh on its own, but will miss the Building Laugh waiting for them when P-A-C-E rolls one directly into another, each generating a bigger and bigger Button by the rest of the cast – and thus the audience, just like a triple laugh line.

Wait for your laughs, of course - - but the rest of the time: P-A-C-E,  P-A-C-E!!

*

In a comedy, **keep your voice clear and open,** assuring the audience that all is well and that, though they (and the characters on stage) are going to be subjected to all manner of rigors or adversity this evening, the aspects of the conflict will make them laugh, moment by moment, and of course revel in the ultimate happy resolving of it all. Tightness of jaw and vocal production might work in DRACULA, but not in PRIVATE LIVES.

*

## Comedy calls for Curvilinear Visual Lines.

When you walk, or when you throw a prop, always CURVE the move, never approaching a piece of furniture in a straight line, or throwing something directly at a person.  Toss an object in a gentle Arc, and Bend the progress of your walk as if tracing the path of a roulette ball around its wheel.

Use straight lines in a comedy only for breaking the mood.

*

One of the secrets of Comedy is to **Speed Up Transitions**.

Remembering that audiences travel on Transitions, and that Transitions are the bases for the emotional life of your character, you can't discard them, and must always keep them solidly in your focus.  But, for the sake of comedy, just accelerate the Reception-Digestion-Reaction.

e.g. In a drama, seeing the dead man on the sofa stuns you, so you can't transition Quickly into the new emotion of Fear, or you'll get an unwanted laugh. You have to take a good few seconds to Absorb what you're seeing.

But in a comedy, where the laugh is wanted, you should make your transition full but Fast.  Receive the information – the sight of the body – and then Digest it more quickly than in a drama – What?!  A Corpse!!! – and plunge immediately into your Reaction – Hysteria!!  Wahhhh! - and the audience will travel with you, enjoying your true-but-rapid comic transition, and anticipating new laughs to come.

*

## Even in drama, there are laugh lines. LOOK for them.

Activate them. In a classical tragedy such as 'the Scottish play' (See Chapter 18) there's the Porter scene, full of humor, well designed by Shakespeare to lighten the bloody atmosphere for awhile.  And I've seen productions of "Medea," "King Lear," and "Othello," in which well-crafted comic scenes, or lines of dialogue, legitimately given us by the playwright, were rewarded with hearty laughter from an audience grateful for the relief.

*

# Chapter 15

# The performance

Professional theatres under union rules only require the actors to check in one half-hour before show time (And indeed that's the name given to this specific time: "OK, Cast. That's it. Go home. <u>Half-Hour</u> tonight is at 8 p.m.")

If that's your call time, Half-Hour, or if your theatre requires the cast to arrive an Hour before the performance starts, but **<u>you've found that it takes you an hour-and-a-half</u>** to get made-up, and dressed, and your hair fixed – and to Prepare – then you very simply must **<u>get to the theatre earlier</u>**. The best theatre companies insist that the curtain go up at the advertised time, and <u>you</u> can't be the person delaying the show.

People who do that are called "divas" or "prima donnas," or worse. And that's <u>not</u> you, right?

*

**<u>Warm Up before each performance</u>** (and each rehearsal). Athletes do, and the work you're going to do in the next few hours is very often more grueling and requires more of your instant control than is required by many sports.

Some theatres, some directors, choreographers and vocal directors will insist on the entire cast warming up together, so they know it's been done right, in communion with the whole ensemble.

If your show doesn't mandate this, then you yourself must spend ten minutes, at least, stretching your body and opening your throat, so all the tools you need will be at your disposal when you need them. Here's an easy and useful warming-up exercise:

**<u>Increase tension to release tension</u>**. Before you've changed into your first costume: Lie on the floor and Tighten Every Muscle in Your Body. Your eyes and your little toes, included. Extra Tight. Tighter than Tight.

And then s l o w l y release each muscle. Very slowly, at your command. This gets rid of any tension, and gives you the control you'll require of every aspect of your body.

This same idea helps relax your voice. Find a corner from where the audience can't hear you, and say aloud, very slowly, with a tightened throat and clenched jaw: "Ninety-Nine," and then open your throat and unclench your jaw, and say it again, smoothly, as illustrated in Chapter 12.

And Yawn a lot. Big, maw-stretching Yawns. Clear the passageway.

*

### Attention to Detail is the mark of the consummate artist in any field, and certainly in a theatre performance.

Audiences are immediately aware of errors of Omission as well as those of Commission. Sure, they see you inadvertently hurting another actor, as happened not long ago in a famous production of "A Streetcar Named Desire," when the actor playing Stanley, throwing the radio out the window, accidentally smashed it into the face of the famous actress playing Blanche. And in a Broadway musical, a well-known actor coming out for curtain call punched the face of a member of the chorus in full view of the audience. The wronged young man protested later that he'd only said, joyfully, "It's a wrap," but the star thought he'd heard something else. The audience was disgusted.

But they *also* notice if you omit something important. Forgetting a flower for your lapel, or a diamond ring, when dialog refers to it, can elicit scoffing laughter, as this lack of Attention to Detail interrupts their tight focus on the unfolding action.

So, before the opening curtain, **at every performance Check Every Detail** involving your character.

Starting with careful knotting of your necktie or making sure both eyes carry the same amount of mascara, you are responsible for every aspect of your costume and make-up, even if you have an expert and attentive crew working with you, and on you.

Be sure that every one of your props is where it should be, on stage, and on each Prop Table. If something's missing, learn that Early, and have it located and put where it's supposed to be.

Take the responsibility, and fulfill every assignment you've been given or have assumed - even if the audience wouldn't know of your involvement – such as handing a prop to an actor who rushes off and right back onto the stage, or holding a flashlight for someone's quick costume change. Your being part of an ensemble also demands total Attention to Detail.

And <u>if the director inserts a new piece of business for you</u>, or you've been given a new costume item, be sure to show the other actors involved, well before Curtain.

*

**<u>The longer the play runs, the sad fact is that it becomes easier for everyone, in the cast and in the crews, to go through the Pre-Show Check-List automatically, almost without thinking</u>.** And of course that's when errors occur, badly weakening your play.

The obvious remedy to that disaster is for each of you, however long your show is open, to religiously and conscientiously follow your pre-show pattern, as soon as possible after you arrive at the theatre, checking the props you'll handle throughout the entire performance and the costumes you'll wear, and allotting enough time for expertly applying your make-up and completing your physical and vocal Preparation.

*

Before the performance, and during each Intermission, **<u>when the Stage Manager gives the Calls</u>**: e.g. "Half Hour" and "Ten Minutes," you must answer her, so she knows you've heard the call. A nod or an unintelligible mutter is not an answer. Worse than either is No Response.

<u>There are Only Two allowable answers</u> to a Stage Manager's Call:

- **"<u>Thank You</u>,"** which means "I've heard you and I'll be ready,"

or

- **"<u>I have a problem</u>,"** which must be discussed at that exact moment.

Such problems may be a missing prop, a damaged costume, or a damaged You – a cut, or a debilitating bruise, or the sudden onset of laryngitis.

**<u>No other answer is acceptable</u>**, and certainly Silence isn't what the hard-working Stage Manager deserves from you. She'd rather hear a cheery "Thank You!"

*

**<u>Perfect your Concentration</u>.** This isn't the same as Listening, though it accompanies Listening.

**Concentration** means Focusing your full attention on each successive moment, your lines, character, emotion and blocking, and the audience interaction with you - to the high degree that you cannot be distracted from your presence on stage by Anything – noises from the street, or audience members whispering to each other, or a piano tipped over in the Wings.

Because, if anything draws you away from the moment, you'll have a hard time regaining your focus, and indeed the audience's focus, too.

To help you achieve this concentration, here's another bit of useful homework you can assign yourself. Play a piece of music, with insistent lyrics – at high volume – while you recite aloud a monologue you've memorized solidly.

Try it again and again, until your focus, your concentration, on your lines (shutting out completely the words and rhythm of the song) is so strong and so complete that you know it can override any distractions when you're on stage.

\*

**Have you ever seen an actor cough or sneeze onstage**, when it wasn't an actual part of stage business? **Probably not.**

And if you HAVE, you can be sure his concentration was faulty, because it's virtually impossible for such "human" foibles to assert themselves into a disciplined and focused performance.

It's along the same lines as a football player being badly injured in the heat of a game, and not realizing it for several minutes. His total concentration on the job at hand (just like an actor) has fired up his adrenalin (just like an actor) and he's unable to allow into his awareness pesky things like a cough or a broken leg (just like an actor). Laurence Olivier once made a list of all his professional injuries; it took an entire page of a book.

I'm not suggesting you put yourself in danger, but that your absolute closing the door on outside cares (and sneezes) is vital to your art and your craft and your believability on stage.

\*

**Act for the audience – not for yourself.**

It's very sad to hear an actor say: "I love rehearsals. I never want them to end." This is the same as an author finding her greatest pleasure in sharpening pencils, or the painter in mixing paint.

Of course, it's wonderful if you enjoy every step of the process, but remember that you, and all who are working on the production, are doing it ultimately for The Audience, one of our two Bosses.

The Rehearsals are certainly a joyful and creative time to dig into your character, reharrowing the inner life and the external traits that make this person different from anyone else, and create the relationships with all the other characters in the play. And it can, and should, be an exciting time of discovery, and the building of a satisfying and workable emotional pattern for yourself within the framework of the production, alongside all your colleagues.

But then – But THEN – in Performance you lay all that work out across the stage, humbly, for the Audience's enjoyment and involvement, because they cumulatively are the Last Actor in the play. Their timing, their reactions, and their silences, tighten or loosen, sharpen or soften, Your timing.

Without them, you have a bunch of people onstage and backstage, working hard to create their Own pleasure – and there's a not-very-complimentary word for that. To offer your almost-finished work of art to the audience, is **What It's All About**, and completes the circle, bringing the final and most necessary fragment into this artistic work.

*

I also despair when I hear an actor say, offstage during a performance: "This audience sucks!" or even "This is a Great audience! They get every reference!" Nay, Nay, good friends, <u>an audience is composed of 300, or 150, or 1000, separate individuals</u>, sitting out there in the House, not totally sure of what to expect when the curtain goes up.

You and the rest of your company will meld them into **An Audience** – or you Won't. The onus lies on You, not on the patrons.

If they fail to react, or react badly, it's not their fault; it means that the performance hasn't engaged them fully enough to turn them from separate beings into one <u>concurrently-responsive Audience</u>. So you as one of the only representatives of the creative team (playwright, director, designers, actors) who has <u>instant access</u> to that audience, that "big black giant who looks and listens with thousands of eyes and ears," as Oscar Hammerstein II put it, had better figure out Why they're still starkly individual non-responders, and do something about it. As ever, you should Intensify the emotions, Tighten the cues, Sharpen the timing of the laugh lines, and fulfill your mission of Wanting to entertain.

Or: <u>If the audience is right with you</u>, laughing when they should, keeping dead quiet (or even quietly sighing) at the dramatic moments, applauding well-delivered speeches and crisply-timed exits, you must remember that they didn't come in out of the rain, or have trouble parking the car, or barely finish dinner, and then just automatically sit down before the show started, and join hands with patrons in the next seats, and declare: "We are an Audience!"

No - YOU caused the remarkable cohesion that structured them into an audience, and that's a tribute to everyone involved with the production.

But now you've got to <u>keep them</u> in cohesion. You can't relax and say, "Oh, Yeah! That's us. We're wonderful!!" No – That way lies failure. Keep your tight focus, maintain the pace that has wooed and won the audience, and say to them, implicitly:

- "You liked Act I? Great! Now we're going to do even better with Act II!"

- "You liked that piece of comedy business? Then watch This one!!"

Never overdoing, never taking them for granted, always working with Their sensibilities in mind.

<u>That's</u> the way to interact with your audience.

*

# Chapter 16

# BE A CONTRIBUTING MEMBER OF THE ONSTAGE TEAM

We're all in this together, onstage and off, and the more we support each other, and the more we **help construct an Ensemble feeling** (as discussed in Chapter 5), the better work we'll do, the better performance we'll give, and the better theatre we'll be offering.

Whether you're playing a scene with a Tony-Award-winning actor, or a beginner performing anonymously under the traditional theatre pseudonym "George Spelvin," you owe each other the courtesy of always being on time, prepared, and very cooperatively eager to share eye-contact and to avoid upstaging.

Too often, an actor with a little more experience - and a lot more ego - than others in the cast will **wrongfully build an imaginary wall around himself**, not trusting the earnest but hesitant acting styles of his colleagues. He'll react, not to the stimuli given him in the dialogue of his supposed onstage partners, but to a stimulus he THINKS he should be given, making his emotions, his movements, too big, too unmotivated by what's actually happening on stage.
And he never gives you eye-contact. He's either too self-assured to want to be brought down by looking into what he considers your weak and helpless gaze, or – more likely – he's afraid to let you see how scared he actually is.

You can tell that I'm urging that **you Not become that selfish person**, no matter how expert and experienced you are.
But if you're saddled with such a sad colleague, the director should be seeing and correcting this behavior. But I hope that you yourself would help bring Mr. Star Performer back into the fold.
An actor I worked with called this the "buy him a beer" approach, meaning that you, or a couple of you with similar feelings, should ask this person out for a hamburger, a cup of coffee, or,

yeah, a beer, after rehearsal, and in the course of the inevitable discussion of "How Do You Think Rehearsals're Going?" bring up the fact that you know you're nowhere near performance-ready, and that you have a lot of work to do, and would be very grateful if he'd give you some suggestions - - - that you think that his greater experience could be a boost to you.

This is not hogwash on your part. You CAN learn great amounts from seasoned actors. But Yes, you are flattering him (sincerely) to get him to come out of his self-built isolation booth and join the rest of you as new-found friends.

It works. And the Ensemble benefits. And the performance benefits. And even Mr. Smart Guy benefits. Win-Win.

*

## Help each other to achieve laughs, earn applause, etc.

Once when I was a theatre student, I was playing Captain Edstaston in Bernard Shaw's comedy, GREAT CATHERINE. This character was a silly-fool Englishman sent to the court of Catherine the Great of Russia, to help unite her country with England in matters of diplomacy.

But her prime minister, Potemkin, wants to thwart the British plans, and his roughshod, often physically intimidating, manners, seen against the prim and proper Edstaston, make for much of the comedy.

I shared a dressing room with the huge actor playing Potemkin, who one night after the show was congratulating himself on all the laughs he'd gotten in that performance. "You mean the laughs WE got," I said. "You say the crude words, but it's my reaction *(my 'button')* that cues the laughs."

No, No, No, he assured me that it was his broad playing of a peasant-in-court-clothing that earned the laughter, and I had nothing to do with it.

"OK," I said, "tomorrow night I won't put a button on your lines, and let's see what happens." He agreed gleefully.

Well, you can guess what happened. He belted out his lines, and waved his arms as always, but I merely looked at him, with my English gentleman's assurance, omitting the looks of distaste, or turning briskly away, or putting my handkerchief to my nose, as I had always done before, to button his funny stuff – and now there were No Laughs.  It really did require Both of Us.

This change in the blocking was unforgivable and a very amateurish prank of mine, and I'm still ashamed of it, and urge you never to so anything like it - - - but I DO urge you to realize, as Potemkin did that night, that the entire performance, and every moment within it, succeeds because of Everyone's participation, as this young actor's undisciplined experiment proved.

Work Together from first rehearsal to the final curtain call on closing night, and it'll be a far better show for the solid cooperation within.

*

**If one of your fellow actors "goes up" on stage, losing her lines** – as can happen to any of us at any time – **Help Her.**

Wait until you're sure she's not "pausing for effect," and until it's evident that she's not going to be able to save herself (Usually made clear by her eyes, which are looking at you in abject horror) and then jump in to save her.

Oh, sure, you'll feel as if you've been dropped into an elevator shaft, and your heart is hovering somewhere around your middle ear, flapping helplessly, but you can save the day by Taking Responsibility.

You certainly know her next line, because it's a cue line for you - so turn it around and reconfigure it to fit into Your Character's mouth and say it loud and clear, as you look unwaveringly at her  – and then say Your Actual next line, which should help her find her pattern.  If not, if she's still lost, do the same with her following line.

While speaking her words, look her straight in the eye – even if you have to take her by the shoulders – with love and support and belief glowing in your eyes, letting her know you're there for her as long as needed.

Take a long, deep breath, and be sure she sees it, and breathes deeply in turn.

These supportive actions should bring her back on board. Until they do, speak up positively, in full projection and in character, as you say the lines of dialogue that aren't being said by the lost soul opposite you.

When you can, catch the eye of everyone else on stage, saying to them silently: "Follow my lead!"

If you can't remember all of the lost actor's lost lines, then Invent some. You remember what play you're in, and what scene you were performing when things went wrong. So re-cap the scene aloud in ad-libbed dialogue, with strength and positivity in your voice, teaming up with everyone else on stage. You know what you're doing – you really do - so Do It!

The audience will never know anything has gone wrong, if you comport yourself <u>with great confidence</u>. Until your partner remembers the next accurate line, make it look as if it's the normal, rehearsed scene, moving as always, so no one out front is aware.

The thing Not to do, of course, is abandon her.

Like you, I'm sure, I've seen some horrible moments of abandonment. In one show, the guy obviously couldn't find his next line, and babbled some half words, to which the actress playing his wife commanded: "Well, Say SOMEthing!" which, naturally, drove him further into the depths of "drying up."

Another time, instead of helping his partner recapture his lost lines, or showing by his eye contact how he was there to help, an actor gave some ill-fitting farewell remarks, and Left the Stage. The stage manager compassionately called the curtain down, saving the poor confused and marooned actor, standing alone and clueless.

<u>To save **Yourself** if you lose your lines,</u> see the Stage Fright entry in Chapter 2.

*

The taboo of **never moving on another person's line, not as much as an eye-lid,** isn't as strict today as it was in Miss Galflong's time, but be selective if you're going to move any part of your body while someone else is speaking, and be careful not to steal focus or break into the audience's attention.

*

**Respect your audience, and your fellow actors.**  In too many theatres, even highly regarded professional institutions, some actors regularly try to <u>break each other up</u>, making faces or carrying the wrong props in a way that the audience can't see them, or whispering disconcerting remarks.

This is often a tendency on Closing Night, when some of the worst offenders even change blocking or dialogue to the amusement of the cast but the total confusion of the audience.  In one performance, actors wrote profanities on their foreheads in lipstick, too small to be read by the audience, but right there for the rest of the cast to see and try to swallow their laughter.

I can't imagine where this tradition was born, but I urge you to not let it infect your theatre.  Closing Night audiences deserve the same fine performances their friends have seen earlier and have told them of, and that they're paying for (if only with eager anticipation and attention).  Your last performance should be your best.

On a Broadway musical that I stage managed, one of the producers, a composer whose work is still famous today, decided that he would engage in this terrible final-performance horseplay, and insert himself onto the stage; he had the Wardrobe Mistress fit him with three different costumes that had been used when needed by understudies, including a woman's dress.  He was the boss, so she did what he asked.  Then he sneaked onto the stage in three musical numbers, frolicking along the sidelines, visibly startling the legitimate singers and actors trying to close out their show professionally.

Not funny, not courteous, and not to be tolerated, even if you're the guy who hired the hall.

Another inexplicable tradition that has been too long allowed to continue at some theatres **is Not saying the last line of the play** until Opening Night.

The long-held mythology isn't done for frivolity, I believe, but as a sincere superstitious gesture toward Good Luck.

The folklore requiring that the final line of dialogue not be uttered in rehearsal is based, I'm told, on fear of over-rehearsing, of peaking too early, and thus bringing to Opening Night an overdone, limp piece of work. It's wrongly said to be similar to the thrilling sound in every French theatre of three loud, resonating beats on the stage floor, just before the opening curtain goes up, to signify the final nails going into the scenery.

Well, come on! The closing line is the last thing the audience will hear; it's the sewing-up of the performance, the cherry-on-top of the evening - - - - and if the actor has never said it before, and the director not heard and approved the way it's said, what kind of under-rehearsed pabulum are we feeding the audience?

Please, see these "traditions" for what they really are: Games that some bored people invented to show off, and to hold onto their thinning attention, when the act of creativity wasn't enough for them.

*

In a contemporary play, some actors, especially those inexperienced on stage, think **they'll just wear their own clothing in performances** – sometimes just whatever they were wearing all day. **Not so.**

First of all, the wear-and-tear on street clothes in a 2½-hour play is grim, because of the energy you're expending. You shouldn't subject your own suits and trousers and dresses to that stress.

But, mainly, the costume designer wants to create a specific 'palate' for this production, and your red tie or purple blouse may clash with the scenery, or with what some of the other characters are wearing. So be glad to have the producers providing your outfits, and wear exactly what they offer you.

*

<u>**Stay Alive every second you're on stage**</u>.  Too many actors go into "neutral" and let the fire grow cold in their bellies when the focus is on other actors, and there's a while before their next lines are due.  Not allowed!!  Remember: **<u>"Acting" is from the Latin</u> <u>"actus"</u> – "<u>doing</u>."**

This doesn't mean to move around or over-react and steal the scene; of course not.  The best way to Stay Alive on stage is to **Listen** actively.

In life, one of the traits that attracts us to an individual, whom we then become friends with, or fall in love with, is that this good person Listens when we speak, not just Hearing us, but Listening to us.

This same trait is necessary for an actor, every moment you're on the stage.  Listening to every word, every sound, keeps you Alive and Vibrant, letting the audience know that your character is involved in the moment, not just waiting for your next line.

It's also a very Practical tool for an actor.  If you're not listening carefully, you're liable to miss another actor's mixing up or dropping a line, and if you just answer automatically as rehearsed, you may confuse or irritate the audience.

If the sequence as written is:
Betty:  *I'm not ready for college.*
Mary:  *What do you mean, you're not ready?*

... but one night, the actor playing Betty develops a glitch in her mind and says erroneously:

*"I'm not <u>going</u> to college."*

And the actress playing Mary, wondering whether she has laid out her next costume in the dressing room, ready for the quick change, isn't listening, but says her rehearsed line:

*"What do you mean, you're <u>not ready</u>?"*

The audience then realizes it's spending its time with ill-prepared actors, and starts looking for the exit.

*

**If you break up on stage** (meaning if you start giggling or laughing out loud – what the British call "corpsing") you'll have lost the audience's attention and respect for the next few minutes, if not for the rest of the performance. **It's amateurish, it's childish, and it's unforgiveable.**

Sure, we all have the urge sometimes to laugh onstage, usually when a fellow actor has said a line wrong, or dropped a prop, or someone in the audience has made a loud inappropriate remark or guffaw – or when a legitimate laugh goes on far too long, and we keep holding, and holding, and holding.  But you can't give way to the beginning of a tickling laugh in your throat and behind your eyes.  No!

How do you prevent it from bursting forth?  You've got to **HURT YOURSELF**, without letting the audience know what you're doing. Bite your tongue or your cheek, dig your fingernails into the palms of your hands, turn your toes under and lean your weight onto them – anything unseen to dissuade the Laughing Genie from getting control of you.

*

In many theatres, on Closing Night there's **a wonderful participatory experience involving the entire cast and crew – Striking the Set.**

And the props.        And the costumes.        And the lights.

Just as the word "strike" is used when you carry a prop offstage, or a song or scene or line of dialogue is cut from the show, so in its larger sense "strike" means removing Everything: taking down the set, washing the costumes, returning the props and furniture to their owners or the Prop Room, and storing the lighting instruments and pieces of scenery in their place of rest until called for in another production. And permanently Striking (into the dumpster) broken or unusable shards of lumber or fabric.

These theatres believe that the show hasn't ended until the stage is absolutely empty, and has been returned to the theatre ghosts of past performances.

It's a wonderful tradition, and a last opportunity for ensemble work, putting the play away, putting it to bed, Everyone Together, cast and crew.

*

A terrible disease in the theatre is called **Ethnocentricity, meaning "my group is better than your group.**"

It can infect a cast, causing them to think that the Prop Crew and Costume Crew are their servants, and can be screamed at when something hasn't been set where it was supposed to be.

It infects the Crews, who curse the actors for not taking better care of the props and costumes.

And it creates an us-vs-them situation in an art form that should always reward Everyone, but can only do that if everyone respects and compliments the work of all.

*

# Curtain Calls

The last moments of the performance, after the last line of dialogue, the last blackout or last closing of the front curtain **– the last images of You that the audience will remember – are of course the Curtain Calls.**

*

A British friend of mine, living in the U.S., went back to England to visit his mother. He took her to the theatre, and afterward sent me a postcard: "Saw 'Hamlet' at the Royal National Theatre. **Curtain calls were sloppy.**"

No matter how masterful the Shakespearean actors were, this was his ultimate impression of the production.

*

**This is your time to say "Thank You,"** to those patient folks who (probably) paid money to see you; who (we hope) sat attentively for several hours, watching you; who (we hope) laughed when you indicated they should, and kept quiet when your demeanor called for it, and applauded when they felt you were worth it.

And now they're (we also hope) applauding non-stop, for you and the rest of the cast, and (though they might not consciously realize it) for the director, the designers, and, Oh, I really hope, for the playwright.

And **it's now your responsibility to Acknowledge that Applause,** with a gracious, smiling bow. A really sincere bow, not a perfunctory nod, or half-way decline of the shoulders. A heartfelt bow that says:

"Oh, Thank You! You're very kind. I know I was a little slow getting started, and I blew a line in Act II, so your appreciation, and even forgiveness, is very welcome. Here, watch, I'm going to bow again, very reverentially, in gratitude for your kindness."

That's the kind of Curtain Call an audience deserves.

## And it's also Their time to say Thank You to You.

You've just been on an emotional journey together, you and the audience, ending in an exciting dramatic (or comic) climax. So they need the closure of applauding you, expressing their sincere gratitude for sharing your talents with them, and finishing off the evening with an active and positive farewell, each to each.

There was a misbegotten movement a few years ago, to eliminate curtain calls. The curtain closed, and the audience applauded, waiting to see the cast – but the house lights came up and the applause dribbled to a halt, and all became silent. And the audience went home, unfulfilled. I suggest that this is wrong-headed and selfish.

*

Most Calls will bring out the cast, just a few at a time, beginning with the smaller roles, and building up to the leads.

Sometimes, in an ensemble production, the entire cast will appear altogether, for a unified bow.

Some directors like the cast to remain *in character*, throughout the Call – the villain is still stern, the ingénue dewy-eyed, etc; while some will ask you to take your bow *as Yourself*, or at least the warm and generous aspect of yourself.

Perhaps your director will stage an intricate Call, almost a playlet in itself, presenting the characters again in choreographed vignettes, attracting some final laughs, or encapsulating the plot in outline form.

No matter what sort of Curtain Call completes your play, always be aware that **it's part of your performance,** to be approached with all the tools of the dedicated actor, including pace, stageworthiness, thoughtfulness toward your colleagues, and, of course, serving dutifully those two masters, The Playwright and the Audience.

*

Receiving **a Standing O** (for "Ovation") **is a thrilling moment in the theatre.**

When an entire audience – or most of them – <u>stands up while they're applauding you</u>, it's the greatest sight and sound you'll ever experience on a stage; it means they liked your performance, and they want to be <u>very sure</u> that you know that.

It makes worthwhile all the hours and all the work, and time away from your family, and lack of sleep, and doubts and fears.  It's truly wonderful.

### And **especially wonderful is a Back-to-Front Standing O.**

When the people in the first couple of rows stand while they're applauding, the audience members further back, seeing other people rising, sometimes feel that they ought to, also, when perhaps they really don't feel like getting up.  So you're never sure, watching the audience stand from Front to Back, how much the Back people have really been coerced into rising.

But <u>when the standing starts in the Back of the House,</u> unseen by the people in the middle and in the front, who rise of their own excited volition, because they *want* to stand and honor you, that's a Back-to-Front Standing O, and that's pure gold.

*

### Always leave them wanting More!

The worst thing you can see, as you take your third or fourth bow, is the *backs* of the audience, as they walk up the aisles toward the lobby, having applauded as much as they felt they wanted to. Death!

The Stage Manager must feel the strength of the applause, and stop the curtain calls before the clapping has tapered off to nothing.  In fact one call *before* that would ideally mark the end of the bows, so the audience is left wanting another, instead of being forced to applaud more than they'd like to.

*

# Chapter 18

# SOME TRUTHS and MAXIMS OF THE THEATRE, to end with

A wise theatre person once said: "Of all the caveats you ever hear from dressing-room philosophers, the one to hold closest to your heart is: **Never BORE nor CONFUSE an audience**." Listen to this admonition, and make it part of your pre-show mantra, when gearing yourself for the performance.

You know how to avoid Boring them. Just keep your actor's energy alive, maintain tight cues and fill the pattern you've rehearsed.

And you won't Confuse them if you are confident in your full understanding and presentation of every word and concept, and speak with clarity and projection.

It's really that simple.

\*

## Declarative sentences need not (Must Not) merely Declare something.

How do you Feel about what your character is declaring?

"I love you." "I hate you." "The British are coming." "I come to bury Caesar, not to praise him." "Mister Roberts is dead."

All are declarative sentences. But woe betide you if you deliver them plainly as such. <u>What do these declarative words make the character - and if you're doing your job correctly, what do they make the Audience - Feel</u>?

Decide, and support and accompany the declaration with its underlying emotion.

\*

You've probably heard <u>the long-held theatre superstition about **"The Scottish Play**."</u> You know, the one with the three witches and the blood spot that won't go away, and the forest that climbs the hill? It's supposed to be terribly bad luck to <u>even say the name of the play</u> inside a theatre, much less quote any of its (very quotable) lines.

I'm not a superstitious person, but in both the productions of ...(this play)... that I've directed there've been horrible accidents on stage, as well as auto wrecks and deaths in the families of some of the actors.

So if ever anyone speaks the unspeakable anywhere in a theatre building, I join the superstitious throngs who require that the rule-breaker pay penance – usually by forcibly leaving the room, turning around three times, spitting over his left shoulder, and quoting from "A Midsummer Night's Dream": "If we shadows have offended. . ."

\*

Most of the very old theatres in London and Paris and New York brag about their **Theatre Ghosts**, presences of long-dead actors who can be felt hanging around backstage, or appearing suddenly in a dark corridor or even amid the audience.

There aren't many tales of <u>malicious</u> spirits; indeed, most of the actors who say they've seen (or "felt") a ghostly visitor claim it was friendly and supportive and contributed to an improved performance on stage.

Even newer theatres have begun describing the existence of something unexplainable backstage.

If you encounter what may be a Theatre Ghost, count yourself lucky, and draw from it its approval, its strength, and its good will, and carry onstage with you these auspicious bonds from an "ancestor" who trod these same boards you're treading and imbues you with its panache.

\*

### Another theatre superstition bans Whistling in the Dressing Room.

I asked a very old actor where this seemingly silly taboo had come from, and he quickly replied: "Actors are terrible whistlers." Well, No, that's not it.

The derivation goes back to the early days of theatre in the United States, when many of the stagehands who handled the flying of scenery up into the fly loft were former seamen, experienced in hauling up sails. The Pin Rail on sailing ships where the ropes were tied off around belaying pins was strikingly similar to the Pin Rail (or Fly Rail) in old theatres, where the ropes, or lines, were held in place by those same Belaying Pins.

There was no intercommunication system in those days, of course, so the ex-sailors would take their cues, as they had on shipboard, by soft whistles from the Stage Manager, who'd replaced the nautical Bos'n. Well, too often someone's jaunty whistle in the dressing room was erroneously heard by the flyman, and down came the castle drop in the middle of the drawing room. So no more whistling.

*

### You're asking for trouble if you believe your Reviews.

Favorable notices in the media may give you an inflated sense of the magnificence of your abilities, which can cause you to become lax in your attention to the details of your work, before and during the show.

And an unfavorable review could hit you hard emotionally, and send you onstage, sadly dragging with you the awful memory of those unflattering remarks – or worse, cause you to change your performance to conform to the ideas of the critic.

A review usually carries a byline, giving the name of its author, which you must recognize only means: "This is One Person's Opinion." Fine. Everyone's entitled to an opinion, but just because this guy's is in the newspaper or on the air doesn't mean it has any more value than your own sense of how you're doing, or your director's notes, which must be of the most importance to you.

So: Never change a Thing in your performance without an absolute OK from your director.

If a critic complains that the whole production is bad, you must still believe in your show, and give it your very best focus and dedicated energies, at every performance.  After all the work you've done in rehearsals (and preparing at home for those rehearsals) you can't abandon the play and your fellow actors now.  Dig in, and make each moment the best you can, and you'll find that the great majority of your audience won't be influenced by any reviews, but will appreciate the fine, hard work of everyone in your theatre.

**The best advice is to Never Read Any Reviews, until after the show has been closed for a week.**  And maybe not even then.

*

In Miss Galflong's day, the snappy, trendy definition of our art form was:  **"Acting is Re-acting."  Well, sure, that's part of it,** for we've seen that a Transition is triggered by, and <u>reacts to</u>, a stimulus.

But if you're discovered onstage at curtain's rise, washing dishes, you don't have much to react to, so this definition, alone, fails at the first moment of the play. No, I refer you to the definition: **"Acting is the portrayal of the inner life of the character, as gracefully and efficiently as possible."**
When the stimuli come, your character will of course <u>react</u>, but you need all the other tools of an actor's technique, too, to attain that grace and efficiency.
Most specifically (as you'll see at the very top of this page): **Acting means Doing!!**

*

**Why is the Green Room called the Green Room**?   That's the name of the backstage area where traditionally the cast and crew congregate when offstage, and, often, meet the public following the performance; the derivation of this name is lost in centuries of stage dust and imaginative memories.

It's frequently said that the walls of the common offstage room were painted green because that was the most soothing color to eyes that had been brutalized by the blazing white limelight used onstage during much of the 18th century to illuminate the actors - produced by the burning of calcium oxide (lime) to an intense degree.  Coming offstage, everyone sought the restful antidote of the green room.

But that can't be right, for the term was in use much earlier.

I prefer this undocumented interpretation:  Among all the dirt-poor actors in a particular 17th-century company, one man – named Green – was recognizably well-off, and always had a bottle or two of alcoholic spirits on hand.  After a performance, the word would often circulate among the cast: "Let's meet in Green's room."

Why not?

*

It's sometimes a good choice to **Play against the obvious**.

Everyone can play Anger by clenching his fists, clenching her jaw, and clenching their eyes into little slits.  Yep, that's Anger.  But, often, if it doesn't work against your character's temperament, I suggest that you try the Opposite.

Portray Anger by being very still, almost deathly, with every muscle relaxed.  Maybe a quiet, smug smile. You'll disarm the audience by Not playing what they expect.

And Fear.  The cliché is to widen your eyes, hunch your shoulders while darting your head around looking for the source of your fright, and breathing heavily and audibly.  But how about approaching it from another angle?  Lift your head courageously, and stand tall and strong.  Only your character's dry mouth and ultra-slow breathing betray your desperate fear.

Try it, with these and other emotions which are sometimes too easy to portray stereotypically.

*

No matter how many roles you've already played, and how many shows of all sorts that you've seen in your lifetime, one of my closing recommendations to you is: **READ MORE PLAYS**!

Haunt the library, read all they've got, and then seek out Other libraries.  Read from all periods of literary history, all nations, all styles.

To prepare for every sort of role you may face in the future, familiarize yourself with the works of as many different playwrights as you can.

And – Yes! - remember that a person in this revered artistic profession is not a "playwrite," but a "playwright," because **plays are not written, they're wrought!**

And they make exciting reading.

Also: **SEE More Plays**!  Locally, regionally, and in the major theatrical centers.

New plays, and new productions of familiar plays. (Someone who says: "I've already seen 'Death of a Salesman,' so I don't need to see it again" betrays stark ignorance, because a new production will have a different director and actors and scenery and lighting, and its fresh concept may evince a whole new response from that 'experienced' theatregoer.)

Watch all the actors closely, in each production you see, discerning their techniques and their truths, their projection of character traits, their handling of blocking.  Learn from their good moments, and perhaps even more from their bad.

But mainly, enjoy the sublime experience of sitting in a theatre alongside dozens of people who, like you, chose to spend this time in this place.  Let the words of the play wash over you, and the sights of scenery/costumes/actors dazzle your eyes, and the emotions driving the plot upward and upward engage your own, as the combination of all these arts and artists carry you away from your daily life – Even Your Life as a Theatre Person – and gift you with the new look at the human condition that, at best, is found at every performance of every play, everywhere.

*

At the end of a long evening of rehearsal, a relatively-new actor, a bright and exuberant middle-aged woman, said to me: "There's just So Much to remember!"

Oh, Yes, there is.

As an actor in the middle of the rehearsal floor the first night you're doing Act I off book. . .

or standing offstage and upstage of a heavy-looking castle door, ready to enter on Opening Night . . .

or leaping onto the third step of a tall curving staircase, halfway through a complicated dance number . . .

you've got an awful lot going through your mind.

## There's just so much to remember!

**SO**: FORGET EVERYTHING YOU'VE READ IN THIS BOOK.

**FORGET IT ALL.    Really.**

Anything worthwhile, any of the techniques discussed here, that you have felt can help you, will stay with you now – indeed, they are already settling themselves into your memory-bank - without your consciously trying to remember them.

And that's Good because, when you're singing an impossibly-complex patter song about Russian composers in "Lady in the Dark," or proclaiming Touchstone's "seventh cause" series of comic polemical arguments, you should NOT be asked to ferret out ephemeral details about foot positions or the terminology of the Lightning Bolt from crevices of your overloaded brain.

Never.

These pages will be waiting for you when you get home from the theatre, to help solve a tricky counter-cross, or remind you how to score a second or third laugh from a single line, or offer a tried-and-true approach to Preparation.

But check out such paragraphs Away from the theatre, when the atmosphere is calm and quiet, and you can decide how much of this advice you want to absorb, and, Yes, how much to ignore.

It's true that **Acting is Not easy**, and I hope you're glad of that fact.  Because if it were easy, then everyone could do it, and it wouldn't be special for us anymore.

- - - - - - - - -

The word "Don't" doesn't ever appear as an admonition in this book, except when quoting someone else. This has been deliberate for, in matters of acting technique, it's wise to avoid saying that word, even to yourself.

It's a Negative, and you should only be carrying onstage with you Positive thoughts and motivations, to encourage you to DO.

Remember what the Romans taught us:

Acting means Doing !!

_____

A last suggestion, regarding all these techniques:

EVERY ONE OF THEM CAN BE **BENT** – or OUTRIGHT **BROKEN, if you know Why** you're breaking it.

Once you, the artist, have learned the Techniques and can perform successfully within them, it's exciting to seek other routes to bring your art to your audience.

Picasso was a superb draftsman, knowing and expertly working within the tenets of the art world of his time, before he went off in his own creative direction to create his cubist masterpieces.

Just remember that you're not a solo artist, but part of an Ensemble, headed by a director whose interpretation of the Playwright's script is shaping the performance - - so your inclination, as a gifted, educated and experienced actor, to bend a conventionally accepted discipline of our art, has to be checked with and approved by your colleagues.  And you have to have a better reason than "It might be fun."

But as long as you thoroughly know and can exemplify the "accepted" ways of an actor's craft, please believe that there're countless byways and tributaries and new worlds awaiting the propulsion of your imagination and talent to discover them and bring them to a future audience.

# <u>Break the Rules!</u>
## (after you've <u>Learned</u> the Rules)

and

# <u>Break a Leg</u>!!!

21862095R00123

Printed in Poland
by Amazon Fulfillment
Poland Sp. z o.o., Wrocław